good news FROM Luke

Visual messages for children

LAVERN G. FRANZEN

AUGSBURG PUBLISHING HOUSE
MINNEAPOLIS, MINNESOTA

GOOD NEWS FROM LUKE

Copyright © 1976 Augsburg Publishing House

Library of Congress Catalog Card No. 76-3869

International Standard Book No. 0-8066-1528-1

Scripture quotations unless otherwise noted are from the Revised Standard Version of the Bible, copyright 1946, 1952, and 1971 by the Division of Christian Education of the National Council of Churches.

MANUFACTURED IN THE UNITED STATES OF AMERICA

Contents

4

To all the kids at Our Redeemer, whose joy in the Good News is a constant thrill;

To those who share the Good News with other kids everywhere;

And to two wonderful teachers, Ted and Dorothy Kollmorgen, who gave this kid that sense of the Good News years ago in a parochial grade school in Leigh, Nebraska.

Preface

Most children learn early in their Sunday school and church experiences that the word *Gospel* is another way of saying *Good News*. Many of our growing-up Christians already know its derivation, along with its definition. It would seem that we're doing an excellent job of sharing that *Good News*.

We'd agree that learning the background of the word is part of thorough instruction; we'd agree as well that defining that *Good News* in God's love for his world, his act to become part of it in Jesus Christ, and his rescue for the world through Christ is the very center of our proclamation of the Gospel.

But we do wonder if our younger hearers can translate that definition into their experiences in much of their church life, or even extract it from those experiences. It is not that our leaders have not proclaimed the Gospel as God's Good News to every human situation; it is that the human situation is most frequently perceived as basically an adult one. We deal most frequently, and sometimes most comfortably and competently, with adult themes, adult problems, and adult vocabularies. It might surprise us to discover that many children feel our adult directed messages are not so much *Good News,* after all.

Yet these smaller sinners must hear the same Good News speaking to the bad situations of their experiences, if their life in Christ is to be anything but a superficial sort of "Jesus Loves Me, This I Know" relationship. (We have nothing against "Jesus Loves Me" but do feel that children are cheated if that is the extent of their relationship with him.)

So these messages, adapted visually from adult proclamations of the very same themes, are meant to say to God's little people that they are part of the world he loves, and just as important in it as those much older. We have tried to say in each message that all ages need his great rescuing work, and the Word and Sacrament in which it is shared. We have tried to say that from Baptism to resurrection, all of us live in the Good News, and find life by it. How successful we have been the reader and user of these materials will have to decide, as each person adapts them for personal use.

One final word: I would be remiss if I did not acknowledge with very sincere thanks all those whose support, encouragement, criticisms, and suggestions have gone into this collection of messages. The joy of the little people of God at Our Redeemer, the suggestions and advice of my wife, Mary Ann, and the response of colleagues have all entered the sort of process from which these messages have come. They represent the goal we have for the messages themselves, the people of God, joined to him and to each other in Jesus Christ, and finding life formed in that *Good News,* whether it comes from Luke, or those who interpret him.

LAVERN FRANZEN

We're Ready

SCRIPTURE

"Now when these things begin to take place, look up and raise your heads, because your redemption is drawing near."

"But take heed to yourselves lest your hearts be weighted down with dissipation and drunkenness and cares of this life, and that day come upon you suddenly like a snare; for it will come upon all who dwell upon the face of the whole earth. But watch at all times, praying that you may have strength to escape all these things that will take place, and to stand before the Son of Man."

Luke 21:28, 34-36 (First Sunday in Advent)

PREPARATION

You will need a flashlight in working condition, but with two sets of batteries, one set of which is dead, the other set working. Label the working set with the words WORD OF GOD and SACRAMENT. Label the non-working set with the words OUR SIN and OUR PRIDE. (Note: These labels should be placed on the batteries in such a way that they can be hidden from the children when they are first shown.)

I have something in my hand which is a very handy thing to have. All of you know what it is, don't you? Of course, it's a flashlight, and I've had to use it several times. One night when I changed a tire on my car I needed it; one evening at home when the lights went out it was useful. A flashlight is a good thing to have.

That is, it's a good thing to have if it's ready to use. *(Flick the light on and off several times to indicate that it is a working light.)* This one works very well, and we know why. It has a good bulb, and it has good batteries. *(Open the light, remove the batteries and show them, being careful not to show the labels you have placed on them.)* If a flashlight is going to be ready, that's what it needs. *(Change the batteries as you speak, replacing the good batteries with the dead cells.)*

You see what happens when the batteries are dead? *(Try the light several times.)* This flashlight just isn't ready at all, is it? And we all know which flashlight we'd want when we needed one, don't we? We want one that is ready. Actually, we want it to be ready all the time, because we never know when we might need it. And if we need the light and it's dead, that's just too bad.

But did you know that flashlights are something like people? They have to be ready, and so do we. We have to be ready for something else though. Jesus tells us that we are to be ready for him when he comes back to us. We don't know just when that will be, anymore than we always know when we'll need this. *(Show the flashlight.)* Sometimes, though, we have our own dead batteries. *(Remove the batteries from the light, this time showing the labels.)* That's right, our sin and our pride can make us feel that we are ready enough, that we don't need anything more to be ready for Jesus' coming back. And if we let them have their way, we might just not be ready.

That's why Jesus came the first time, though. He came to make us ready for him when he does come back. You see, when he suffered and died on the cross to make us his children, he left something for us so that his children could be ready. *(Show the batteries labeled* WORD *and* SACRAMENT.*)* That's right; he left us these. *(Place them in the flashlight, and turn it on.)* And with our new batteries, we have his power over our sin and our pride. With our new batteries Jesus makes us new people waiting for him to come back, because we're ready.

To Turn Us Around

SCRIPTURE

And he went into all the region about the Jordan, preaching a baptism of repentance for the forgiveness of sins.

Luke 3:3 (Second Sunday in Advent)

PREPARATION

Fold a long piece of cardboard approximately fifteen by thirty inches or so lengthwise. On one half of the cardboard mark a series of squares as if you were marking spaces for a game to be played with markers or miniature autos. Label these spaces with words denoting common sins for young people, such as cheating, disobeying, lying, fighting, hating, swearing, etc. In the very last space print the word HELL. On the opposite side of the cardboard, mark off spaces to correspond, and label each space with words indicating Christian action, such as loving, helping, obeying, telling the truth, studying God's Word, etc. (The number of spaces is limited only by the size of your cardboard and the type of marker you will use. See next paragraph.) Mark the last space HEAVEN.

For markers you may use the common small markers many children's games provide. More effective, though, is the use of a small toy automobile.

This looks something like one of your games, doesn't it? *(Show the board you have made, with the side demonstrating the sins toward the children.)* Maybe it is; at least, it's like what we might call the game of living. So let's look at it very carefully, and pretend we're playing that game of life this morning.

This is the way life sometimes is. We move along from one thing to another. *(Move the marker.)* But it's sad that the things we move to aren't always such good things for us. Let's look at some of them. *(Read them aloud, or permit the children to do so, moving the marker from one place to another as you do.)* Those are not such good things for us, are they? They are just the opposite of the way God would like his children to be, just like this place is the opposite of the place God would want his children to live. *(Point to the word* HELL. *Note: Both this space and the corresponding space on the other side can be omitted if you choose. If you use them, be very careful not to let them see the consequences of the other spaces, as if cheating always leads to hell, or loving leads to heaven.)*

But the sad part is that that's the way we are. By ourselves it just seems that this is the way we play the game, and we can't even stop ourselves. *(If you are using a toy auto, place the car at the beginning of the spaces, and tilting the board, let the auto roll downward, stopping it at the end.)* We would be just like this car, and we'd go right off the edge, if nothing stopped us.

But we're God's children, and we do have some good news because we are. God tells us we don't have to play this game on this side at all. He sent Jesus into the world to turn us around. *(Turn the board over so the opposites show.)* Jesus made all our sins like *(name those you have on the board)* his very own, so that he could give us a new life with new ways to live. He turns us from being hating people to being loving people. *(Continue with the other parallels you have mentioned.)* And finally, he tells us that we will live with him in heaven forever. *(Point to the word.)* That's really turning things around, isn't it!

And that's what a word in today's Gospel meant, when we heard that John came preaching a baptism of repentance. Repentance means turning around, and that's what Jesus does for us. When we were baptized, he turned us around to play this kind of life. *(Indicate that side of the board.)* Without him, we'd be like this *(show the sins)*, but with him, we're turned around.

The Right Kind of Fruit

SCRIPTURE

Bear fruits that befit repentance, and do not begin to say to yourselves, "We have Abraham as our father"; for I tell you, God is able from these stones to raise up children to Abraham.

Luke 3:8 (Third Sunday in Advent)

PREPARATION

You will need several empty fruit or vegetable cans and several grocery items which will seem to be almost completely opposite in taste. For example, in a can labeled "peaches" you might place an onion, or in a can labeled "applesauce" you might place a cucumber. Your choices are immaterial, but the more they can seem to be directly opposite, the more effective the presentation will be.

Make a new label for one can. (If you choose, and have either time or artistic inclination to do so, use a box covered to give a representation of a church for this part of the lesson.) Inside this place slips of paper with the following texts:

1. I am a member of _____ church.
2. I go to Sunday school all the time.
3. I give a lot of money, so I'm good.

Also, in the same can or box place a cross (made of cardboard if no other is available) and a heart.

How many of you have gone to the grocery store with your parents? Of course, most of you have. And we all know that when you buy your groceries you expect them to be what the label says, don't you? For example, this is a can of peaches. *(Show the can.)* What do you think it will have in it? *(Wait for the answer, and then respond conversationally.)* But let's see. Look at this. *(Show the onion.)* Well, that's a lot different, isn't it? That would make a funny dessert, if you wanted to serve peaches and ice cream, and instead opened up to find onions. You'd know something was wrong.

Or look at these. *(Demonstrate the same point with the*

other cans you have prepared, involving the children con-
versationally as you do. Note: There is a certain amount of
humor in this lesson. Care must be taken that it does not
get out of hand, so that the viewers remember the humor
rather than the point.) It's really the same with all of
these, isn't it? We looked at the label and expected to see
something, but instead we saw something different.

Now let's look at this. What does this label say? *(Wait*
for the response that it is labeled "the church.") Now let's
see what's inside. We'd expect it to be filled with people
who love Jesus and who love each other, wouldn't we?
But let's see.

(Begin drawing out the slips of paper.) It looks like
something is wrong here, doesn't it? Something is wrong;
something is really wrong. Instead of people who are
showing they are God's people by their love, these are
things like people being proud because they are members
of this congregation, or people thinking they are better
because they go to Sunday school all the time, or because
they give more money. It is good to be here with God's
people in this congregation, and it is good to be in Sunday
school and church, and it is good to be able to give money
to help teach about Jesus. But that's not the thing that
makes us his people. Maybe we'd better look again.

Here it is; this is what we're really looking for in the
church. *(Show the cross.)* That's the sign of the church,
really. It's the cross, and we know that Jesus suffered and
died on it to make us his people. We're here because of
what he did for us, and what he does for us with his
Word. But then, maybe we can even look again to see
what's inside the church when Jesus is with us. And here
that is. *(Show the heart.)* It's his love, and it means our
love for each other, too. And when God's people live with
his forgiveness *(show the cross)* and his love *(show the*
heart) and forgive and love each other, then the label
"church" is right, and we're producing the right kind of
fruit. We don't have the labels mixed up any more.

His New Building Blocks

SCRIPTURE

He has shown strength with his arm, he has scattered the proud in the imagination of their hearts, he has put down the mighty from their thrones, and exalted those of low degree; he has filled the hungry with good things, and the rich he has sent empty away.

Luke 1:51-53 (Fourth Sunday in Advent)

PREPARATION

You will need a shallow cardboard box and five children's building blocks, of sufficient size so they can be stacked one on top of the other, and yet not so large that they will fall out of the box when they are toppled.

Label the blocks with the letters P-R-I-D-E, and on the other side, label them with the letters L-O-V-E. Label the final one with a cross.

Christmas is almost here, isn't it? I imagine we're all very excited about it, because Christmas means so many good things. It means Christmas carols and special programs and Christmas cards and candy and presents, too. We're really excited about all those things, aren't we? *(You may easily get so much response on this that you will have to be ready to interrupt it.)* But most exciting of all is that we're going to be celebrating Jesus' birthday.

That's why I have this box to show you. *(Demonstrate.)* I call this my "Jesus birthday box" and I'll show you why, in just a little while. But first I want to show you something else. I want to show you how we can get all mixed up about Jesus' birthday, and fill his birthday box with the wrong things.

For one thing, we talk about getting so many presents, more than anyone else. *(Place the "E" block in the box.)* Or we talk about getting new clothes, better than any others. *(Continue with the "D" block.)* Or maybe it's that

16

we get more money, or a bigger bike, or a bigger box of candy. *(Continue with each example, placing the blocks until they form the word* PRIDE.*)* But do you see what we have now? Instead of being a Jesus birthday box, this is a box which is filled with our own pride. And being proud isn't such a good way to get ready for Jesus' birthday, is it? He didn't come to make us proud; he came for another reason, and that was to take our sins and our pride away. The Bible even says that he came to scatter the proud in all those things they imagine. *(Topple the little tower of blocks you have made as you say these words.)*

But the good news God tells us is that Jesus didn't just come to scatter us because we're so proud. He came to do something else, and that is to gather us to himself in a different way. Jesus was born for us to make us his children, and to give us something in place of our pride. *(Begin rebuilding the stack of blocks, so that it will spell the word* LOVE, *with the cross as the bottom block.)* What word is it? That's right, it's the word LOVE. But love is more than just a word. It's the gift Jesus gives all of us. It's the way he lived for us, and it's the reason he suffered and died to save us. *(Point to the cross.)* He scattered us from our pride, so he could put us together again with his love. And when we live with his love, we're like new building blocks, all because of his birthday.

He Makes Room

SCRIPTURE

And she gave birth to her first-born son, and wrapped him in swaddling clothes, and laid him in a manger, because there was no place for them in the inn.

Luke 2:6 (Christmas Day)

PREPARATION

For this message you will need several symbols of the Christmas season. These might be Christmas cards, a small wrapped package, an ornament from a Christmas tree, a small auto, and either a small manger and infant, or perhaps one of the small one-piece nativity scenes available from a local variety store. You will also need a box, not quite large enough to hold everything.

Today is an exciting day, isn't it! Just think, it's finally Christmas Day, and we have so much to celebrate. But we know why we're here, don't we? We're here because we're celebrating Jesus' birthday. *(Show the nativity scene or manger and infant.)* I wonder who would like to tell me about this? *(Wait for response, and with the help of a few questions, assist the children in telling the Christmas story.)*

Now, I wonder who can tell me where Jesus was born? That's right, he was born in a stable, and when he was born, his mother wrapped him up and placed him in a manger, a place for feeding cattle or horses or donkeys. But that's really different, isn't it? He didn't have a baby bed or anything. He just had this. *(Show the manger.)* And do you know why? *(Wait for response, helping if necessary, so that someone answers, "There wasn't any room for him.")*

That's really sad, isn't it. Just think, there wasn't any room for him. I think we would all have found a place for him, all right, don't you think?

18

But it's still sad that even at Christmastime we don't always find room for Jesus. Things get in the way. *(Begin filling the box with the other symbols of the season.)* We've been so busy writing Christmas cards that we didn't always have time to be at church; that meant we didn't have room. We had to decorate the Christmas tree instead of attending Sunday school; again, we didn't have room. There were so many places to go *(show auto)* that we didn't have time to read God's word or to pray. We didn't have room. We even got so excited about giving and getting presents that we spent more time and money for them than for anything else. *(By this time the box should be full, so that there is no place for the nativity scene.)* But do you see what happened? We were so busy with everything else that we didn't make room for Jesus. There's just no place in our Christmas box for him.

That's too bad, isn't it? And it really would always be bad news except for one thing. Jesus didn't let that stop him. Even when there wasn't room in the inn at Bethlehem, he was born anyway. That's how much he loves us; he still makes room for himself. He was pushed out to a manger, but he came anyway, making room. When he died, he was pushed up on a cross, but even with that he was making room, making room for all of us with his forgiveness.

And that's what we're really celebrating this morning. We're celebrating a God who loves us so much that he makes room to be born for us, and we're celebrating something else, too. We're celebrating his forgiveness, because that's the way he makes room for us to be with him. And that's a good way to say Merry Christmas, because we have a Jesus who makes room. *(Place the nativity scene on top of the box, with everything else around it.)*

Lost and Found

SCRIPTURE

Lord, now lettest thou thy servant depart in peace, according to thy word; for mine eyes have seen thy salvation which thou has prepared in the presence of all peoples, a light for revelation to the Gentiles, and for glory to thy people Israel.

Luke 2:29-32 (First Sunday after Christmas)

PREPARATION

There are no special materials needed for this message, since it is primarily an audience involvement approach.

This morning I'm going to task all of you to help me with our sermon. And to do that you'll have to show me some feelings by the way you look. First, let's practice a little bit. Show me a happy face, please. *(Wait for the response and then comment about it, perhaps indicating how you knew it was happy.)* Now, can you show me a sad face? *(Follow the pattern as indicated previously.)* Show me how you looked when you got a favorite Christmas present; now show me how you might have looked if you broke it. Very good; I can really tell by your face how you feel.

Now, I want you to think about something. Have you ever been lost? Think about how you would feel if you were lost, and then show me with your face. *(Wait for response.)* That's right; you are showing me sad faces, because to be lost is something sad. But now show me how you felt when you saw father or mother. *(Again, wait, and comment.)* That's right again. To be found is something happy, especially when we've felt so sad about being lost.

But now show me something else. You see, we're all sinners, aren't we? That means we don't do the things we are supposed to do; it means we have lost the way to do good things. Show me how you feel when you remember that you have lost God's way. That's right; it's really something to make us sad. But God has good news for us. He didn't want us to stay lost, so he sent Jesus to find us. And Jesus found us by taking our sins away from us. Now show me how you feel when you remember that Jesus has found you. *(Wait once more for response.)*

But that's only part of the good news we have. Even when we have some troubles and feel like we're all alone and almost lost *(indicate with your own expression)* then Jesus tells us that he is always with us, finding us. *(Indicate your own joy facially.)*

So, show me once more. First of all, show me how you would look being lost. *(Wait a proper time.)* And now show me how you can look, since Jesus found you.

The Light Stays On

SCRIPTURE

In him was life, and the life was the light of men. The light shines in the darkness, and the darkness has not overcome it.

John 1:4-5 (Second Sunday after Christmas)

PREPARATION

You will need a flashlight with a strong, bright beam, and four squares of paper marked as follows:

1. I don't have enough time for Sunday school.
2. I want the biggest piece of candy.
3. I hate you!
4. I don't care what Dad said, I'm going anyway.

You will also need a cross, preferably one which you can wear around your neck.

This morning I'm going to ask you to pretend that this isn't a flashlight at all. Pretend that this represents Jesus, and the light coming from it is just like his love. *(Shine the light so the beam touches the face of all the children briefly.)* Can you see it? Of course, you can. And that's really the way we are; we are God's children, and Jesus shines his love on every one of us, just like this bright light. The Bible even tells us that Jesus is the light of the world, and it says, too, that the darkness can't ever stop him.

Sometimes, though, we do like to cover up Jesus' love, or at least it seems that way. For example, whenever we get up on Sunday morning and are all grumpy and crabby about going to Sunday school *(show the paper and permit one of the children to read it)* like this, we're covering up his love. *(Hold the paper in front of the light, keeping the light on, but keep the paper there as well.)* Or whenever we insist that we want the biggest piece of candy, we are being very selfish, and that covers up Jesus' love, too.

(Repeat, with that paper.) Here's another way we cover up his love. *(Show the "I hate you!" paper.)* And here's another. *(Show the last one, with appropriate comments.)* But do you see what has happened to our bright light? It just isn't as bright, is it?

But the Bible did say that the darkness couldn't overcome Jesus' light. And it didn't. Jesus came to suffer and die on the cross *(show the cross)* just to keep his love shining for us all the time. His love is so great and bright for us that he takes these things *(indicate the papers)* away with his forgiveness. They can't overcome his light. *(Crumple the papers and put them aside.)* He crumpled up all their power, just so we can live in his love.

Of course, we all know that on one day it did seem like his light would be gone. That's the day he died, when it seemed like it would all be turned off. *(Turn off the flashlight.)* But even something as dark as a grave couldn't overcome Jesus; he came out of it, and his love is just as bright as ever. *(Turn light on, again playing the beam against the face of each child.)* And that's our good news for God's children. His light stays on!

We're Like Him

SCRIPTURE

Now when all the people were baptized, and when Jesus also had been baptized and was praying, the heaven was opened, and the Holy Spirit descended upon him in bodily form, as a dove, and a voice came from heaven, "Thou art my beloved Son; with thee I am well pleased."

Luke 3:21-22 (The Baptism of Our Lord; Epiphany I)

PREPARATION

Using a shoe box or something of similar size, construct a replica of a church, with arched windows and possibly a steeple. (This need not be an artistic project; the imagination of young minds is fertile enough to supply details older minds often do not.) In the box place a dollar bill, a music book, a Sunday school leaflet, pictures of people praying, and, if available, pictures of people in various kinds of need. If these pictures are not available, or even if they are but you choose to use something else, include a piece of bread, a bottle for medicine, and a small item of clothes.

Today the church remembers something that happened to Jesus, something that happened to all of you, as well. I wonder if anyone knows what we are talking about. *(Wait for response and, if possible, help lead the responses to the answer: "Jesus was baptized.")* That's right; today we remember Jesus' baptism, and, of course, we remember our own, too. When we were baptized, Jesus made us his children, and that's something to remember. We're like him.

There's something else to remember, though, too. For when Jesus was baptized, God said: You are my beloved son; with you I am well pleased. That meant God was happy with the things that Jesus would do.

Now, since we're like him, we really ought to find out what we should be doing, so God could say the same thing

24

about us. Let's look in my church to find out. *(Show the box, and begin taking articles out.)* Now here's something the people of the church do *(show the Sunday school leaflet)* and that's a good thing; we do want to learn more about Jesus. And here's something else. *(Show the money, the music, and the praying, commenting about each, mentioning the value of each.)* All of these are good things, aren't they?

But the sad thing is that so many of us think that's all the church is to be doing. There really is much more. There are things to do just like Jesus did. *(Hold up either the picture of hungry people or the piece of bread.)* Here's something he did; he gave food to the hungry. If we're like him, what do you think we should do? Or here's something else. *(Show the medicine.)* Jesus healed the sick, didn't he; how can we do that? *(Wait for responses of help provide medicine, take people to the doctor, pay for medical bills, etc.)* Or here's another thing we might do. *(Again encourage the children to respond.)*

That's right. All of those things are things we are to do, too. It's not really being like Jesus just to stay inside these walls and sing and pray; there are people who need us and our help. And that's why Jesus came to us in the first place. He came to help us, to feed us with his love and to heal us with his forgiveness, to give us new clothes of a life like his. And because we have them, we are like him, and because we are like him, we can do the things he does. And then we can be as loving and forgiving and helping as he would like us to be. After all, we are like him!

What Jesus Showed

SCRIPTURE

This, the first of his signs, Jesus did at Cana in Galilee, and manifested his glory; and his disciples believed in him.

John 2:11 (Second Sunday after the Epiphany)

PREPARATION

Cut three holes in the bottom of a box so that three water glasses can be set through them. Then trim the sides of the box so that it will fit on a tray, and when inverted, with the glasses right side up, you will be able to pour water in them, but the bottom of the glasses will be hidden from view. Pour a small amount of red food coloring in the second glass, and a small amount of green in the third. You will also need a pitcher of water. (Note: It is really better to have another adult assisting with this message. He should hold the tray high enough so the children cannot see the bottom of the glasses, but still can observe the effect.)

We're going to do a little bit of magic this morning, so I'd like all of you to look at this pitcher very carefully. What do you think it has in it? *(Someone will probably guess immediately.)* Well, let's see. *(Pour some water into the first glass, the one with no food coloring; taste it, or give it to one of the children to taste.)* That's right; it's water. It looks like water, and it tastes like water. That's what it must be. So, let's pour some water for a few more of us. *(Pour some in all three glasses, making appropriate comments as you do.)*

Now, how do you suppose that happened? *(Again, permit the children to suggest some answers.)* Well, you're right, really. The glasses weren't empty; it just looked like they were, and I'm not really a magician at all. If I could really do that trick, though, you'd probably believe I was, wouldn't you! But you see, this wasn't even magic; there is an explanation for it, and I wouldn't want you to believe something that isn't true.

But the Bible does tell us about a time Jesus did something like this. He turned a whole lot of water into wine when people at a wedding ran out of it. But that wasn't magic either; that was a miracle, and when Jesus did it, he showed that he was the son of God, so that people could believe in him, and the Bible tells us that they did.

You see, at that time they didn't know much else about him; the miracle helped people believe in him.

That's where we have something better. We don't have to say to Jesus that unless he does miracles for us we won't believe in him. We don't have to tell him that unless he does all the things we want, he can't be our Savior. He has done the greatest miracle of all times when he suffered and died and came out of the grave again. And he still does a miracle for us, when he shows himself to us in the bread and wine of the sacrament, and in the good news of his Word. That's the way he shows himself to us yet, so that we can be like the first disciples, and believe.

I'm Free! I Can See!

SCRIPTURE

> And he stood up to read; and there was given to him the book of the prophet Isaiah. He opened the book and found the place where it was written,
> "The Spirit of the Lord is upon me,
> because he has anointed me to preach good news to the poor.
> He has sent me to proclaim release to the captives and recovering of sight to the blind,
> to set at liberty those who are oppressed,
> to proclaim the acceptable year of the Lord."
>
> Luke 4:16-19 (Third Sunday after the Epiphany)

PREPARATION

> You will need the cooperation of one of the adults of the congregation to hold the arms of the child. You will also need a large cloth to be used as a blindfold.

This morning I need someone to help me share our word of God. Who would like to help? *(Choose a child old enough not to be disturbed by being held very tightly and being blindfolded.)* And now, I also need someone else to help me, someone grown up. *(Indicate with a nod or some signal that the adult you have chosen should come to the front.)*

You see, when God made us, he wanted us to be happy, loving, free people. Jimmy, can you show me by waving your arms how freedom feels? *(Wait for Jimmy to wave his arms.)* Very good; that's a feeling of freedom, isn't it? And God also wanted us to see his love in everything. Maybe you could show me some action of looking for God's love. *(Demonstrate by opening your own eyes wide, putting your hand over them to shade them, or some similar action.)* Very good. That's the way God meant us to be.

28

But sadly, something happened to us. That something was our sin. When the first people disobeyed God, they changed life for all of us. Now instead of being free people, we are held tight by our sins. *(Wait for the adult to hold Jimmy's arms; you should have instructed him before in this action.)* Jimmy, your arms aren't free now, are they? That's like sin, keeping us from doing good things. And we can't even see God's love all the time either, because of our sin. *(Wrap blindfold on Jimmy.)* It's like being blindfolded. And that's not a very happy way to be, is it, Jimmy?

But as we said, God wants us to be his happy people, and to see his love around us and do loving things for the people near us. That's why he sent Jesus into the world to take our sins away. Now we don't have to have our blindfolds on any longer; Jesus took them away with his love. *(Remove the blindfold.)* Our sin is forgiven and we can see. And we aren't held tight in those sins any longer, either. *(Release the man's hands from Jimmy's arms.)* We are free of them. And do you know, that's exactly what the Bible said in today's Gospel. It said that Jesus came to bring liberty to the captives *(act it out by grabbing Jimmy one more time and then releasing him)* and to give sight to the blind. *(Act this out with a quick action of blindfolding and then removing it.)* That's the good news of what Jesus did for us! We are free, and we can see!

That's Hard to Believe

SCRIPTURE

And he began to say to them, "Today this scripture has been fulfilled in your hearing." And all spoke well of him, and wondered at the gracious words which proceeded out of his mouth; and they said, "Is not this Joseph's son?" And he said to them, "Doubtless you will quote to me this proverb, 'Physician, heal yourself; what we have heard you did at Capernaum, do here also in your own country.' " And he said, "Truly, I say to you, no prophet is acceptable in his own country."

Luke 4:21-24 (Fourth Sunday after the Epiphany)

PREPARATION

Using light cardboard and some yarn, make a set of signs to hang over the necks of some of the children. Use your own ideas for these signs, perhaps relating them to the children you know will be present. Suggestions might be:

I like dolls.

I can throw a football.

I'm a good singer.

Be certain to have these two:

I'm a child of God.

I can forgive your sins.

I will die to forgive you. (Hold this sign back until you use it.)

(As the children come forward, hand the signs to them, helping them slip them over their heads. Then have them line up, facing the others.)

This morning I have some signs we're going to read, signs that tell us about our friends. For example, look at this one. *(Motion to the first child and with the other children, read the sign aloud.)* That's right; it tells us that Susan likes dolls. That's easy to believe, isn't it? We all know Susan, and we know that she does like dolls. Or here's another. *(Motion to another child and again read the sign, making appropriate comments. Be certain to end with the phrase "and that's easy to believe, isn't it?")*

But what about this sign? *(Have the child wearing "I'm a child of God" step forward.)* Do you think this is right? Of course it is; Heidi is a child of God. She was baptized right here in this very church, and baptizing makes us God's children. Sometimes that's a little harder to believe about ourselves, but it is true, and we could all wear this sign. *(Point to the sign Heidi is wearing.)*

But what about this one? *(Indicate the child wearing the sign "I can forgive your sins.")* Do you think Johnny can forgive our sins? *(Permit children to respond, and perhaps even extend the conversation if they do respond freely.)* Well, let's think about it. Johnny can forgive us when we do something wrong to him, can't he? If I hurt him and tell him I'm sorry, Johnny could say, "That's okay. I forgive you." That's not so hard to believe, is it?

Now let's look at this one. *(Show the sign "I'll die to forgive you.")* Suppose we put this one on Johnny; how would we feel about that? You're right. That would be harder to believe. After all, why should Johnny love us that much that he would want to die for us? It really is hard to believe.

But that's just what Jesus did for us. He wanted to make us his children *(indicate sign "I'm a child of God.")* and he wanted to forgive our sins. *(Indicate that sign.)* So he came into the world to be someone just like us. People didn't even know that he was different, at first. But he came to die for us, to take away our sins. We can't be that loving, I don't think; it would be very hard. But he loves us that much. He even takes away the sin of finding it hard to believe!

Going Fishing

SCRIPTURE

And Jesus said to Simon, "Do not be afraid; henceforth you will be catching men." And when they had brought their boats to land, they left everything and followed him.

Luke 5:10-11 (Fifth Sunday after the Epiphany)

PREPARATION

Prepare four fishing poles, using light sticks. (Kite sticks work very well, but even soda straws can be used.) Fashion hooks from paper clips, to hook into the hooks you will place on the fish, or if available, use some small magnets on the fishing line. Out of cardboard or construction paper, cut four fish, to be labeled as follows:

Lots of money
A big house
An important job
People for Jesus

Place these fish in a box, along with a cross.

This morning we're going fishing! That's really something, isn't it? Here you thought you were coming to church, and instead you're going to do some fishing. Well, let's look! Here are the poles *(indicate them)* and here is our fishing pond. *(Hold the box up high enough so none of the children can see into it.)* So let's choose some fishermen, and see what they can catch. *(Pick one child after another, and place the first three fish listed above on their respective hooks. Make appropriate comments during the process, since it should not be done in silence. You might like to use the following as a model.)*

Let's see Terry's fish! It's a good one, all right! And let's see what kind of fish it is; after all, fishermen always like to know what they catch. *(Hold up fish.)* Well, this is the kind a lot of people really fish for all their lives. They like to have lots of money, and that's the reason they do everything.

Let's look for another fish! *(Choose another child, and fasten on the second fish.)* Well, here's another kind of fish, and this one is a big house. That's right, too, isn't it? A lot of people fish for big houses. That's the most important thing in their lives.

Here's another fisherman. *(Give the fishing rod to another child.)* Let's see what Debbie can catch. Oh, oh, she's got one. *(Place the fish labeled "an important job" on the line.)* Now we'll see this one. It's an important job, and that's another real fish for many people. We think that having an important job is the most important thing we can do. How about that?

I wonder if there are any more fish in here. Would someone else like to try? *(Choose another child, and place "People for Jesus" on the hook.)* Now let's see this fish. It says, "People for Jesus," and that's something really different, isn't it? How could we catch people for Jesus? *(If possible, lead children to responses of "Telling about him," or "Bringing someone to Sunday school," or some similar responses.)* That's right; those are ways we can be fishers for people.

But the sad thing is that so often our other fishing gets in the way. *(Indicate the other fish.)* These become so important to us that we forget about this. *(Indicate the last one.)* And that's why we need this. *(Show the cross.)* That's a different kind of fishing pole, isn't it? It's the way Jesus caught us away from our sins and made us his children again, and it's the way he forgives us. He came fishing for us when he was born and when he suffered and died and when he came out of the grave. And the good news we can share is that he takes our sins away and sends us to be fishers for him, not for these *(show the first fish)* but for this. *(Show the one marked "People for Jesus.")*

No Reason to Be Mixed Up

SCRIPTURE

And he lifted up his eyes on his disciples, and said: "Blessed are you poor, for yours is the kingdom of God. Blessed are you that hunger now, for you shall be satisfied. Blessed are you that weep now, for you shall laugh. Blessed are you when men hate you, and when they exclude you and revile you, and cast out your name as evil, on account of the Son of man! Rejoice in that day, and leap for joy, for behold, your reward is great in heaven; for so their fathers did to the prophets."

Luke 6:20-22 (Sixth Sunday after the Epiphany)

PREPARATION

From a newspaper or a catalog, select items which would appeal to children and clip them out for display to the group. Also clip out a large number of different prices, being careful to select prices which vary greatly from the actual price for the items you have chosen. For example, connect a bicycle with a price tag of $.10 and a candy bar with a price of $79.95. (You may wish to use actual items with which the children would be familiar such as a pack of gum, a new baseball glove, a wrist-watch, a transistor radio, a candy bar, a comic magazine, etc.)

You will also need a wallet with several dollar bills in it and a full-page grocery ad, plus a Bible and a cross, neither of which is to have price tags attached.

This morning I'm going to show you some things that all of us like. We really enjoy having these things, don't we? *(Show several of the items you have selected; you may wish to engage the children in conversation about them for a brief time.)* Of course, if we want these as our own, we have to buy them, don't we, or perhaps have someone buy them for us. So let's look at something; let's look at what they cost. *(Begin demonstrating the items, with the prices you have attached to them.)*

Here's something! A bicycle *(or whatever item you choose)* and it's only a dime; how about that? And here's a candy bar, for seventy-nine dollars. *(Draw some comments from the children as you display the items. If they do not volunteer that the prices are wrong, help them to notice it.)* There really is something wrong with all this, isn't there? The prices are all mixed up. The things that really are valuable have low prices, and the things that aren't worth much cost a lot.

Life would be funny if everything would be mixed up like that, wouldn't it? But let me show you something else that gets all mixed up, and this is not funny at all. *(Show the wallet.)* Here is something that many people think is the most important thing in life. Of course we like to have enough of it, don't we? And we can thank God that he gave us enough. But that doesn't mean we should think it's the most valuable thing in the whole world. That would be mixed-up thinking, and just living for money is really mixed-up living. Or here is something else. *(Show the food advertisement.)* This is the most important and most valuable thing for many others. But that's really mixed-up too. Whenever we spend all our time and all our energy and all our activity just at getting these things, we're putting the wrong price tags on them, too.

That's just another of the reasons Jesus came into the world. He didn't want his people living mixed-up lives. He wanted us to have the blessing of living with his word *(show the Bible)* and with his forgiveness. He turns us around from our mixed-up ways so that these can be most important to us. Having a lot of money is nice, but not as important as having his love. *(Show the wallet, and then place the Bible over it.)* Having a lot of food is good, too, but when we're hungry for his love, it's even better. That's why he came *(show the cross),* and because he did, we don't have to be mixed up any longer.

Where People Need Us

And as the men were parting from him, Peter said to Jesus, "Master, it is well that we are here; let us make three booths, one for you and one for Moses and one for Elijah"—not knowing what he said.

Luke 9:33 (Last Sunday after the Epiphany)

PREPARATION

Cut the corners of a shoe box, or a box of similar size, so that you can fold them down easily during the message. (You will probably want to tape them into place lightly for the beginning of the presentation.) On the successive sides of the box, to be legible as the sides are folded down, print the following:

People need us.
People need our love.
People need our help.
People need Jesus.

On the outside of the box with the sides taped back into place print the following:

It's really good to be here.
We can love each other.
We're getting along very well.
Jesus is here with us.

This morning we're going to pretend that this is our church. *(Display the box.)* Of course, our church isn't exactly like a box, but maybe it is in one way. We do have walls just like this box does, and we have a space inside, just like this box. So maybe they are something alike after all. And if this is our church, we can really say these things about it, can't we? *(Indicate the sentences on the outside of the box, turning it around so the children can read one after the other, allowing enough time for some comment and conversation with each one.)*

Do you know, that sounds just like Peter in today's Gospel, doesn't it? He and James and John were with

Jesus on top of a mountain, and it was so nice there with Jesus that Peter wanted to stay there, where there were no problems, just like we might want to stay here in our church for the same reason. But do you know something? Jesus didn't stay there at all. He took the disciples with him and they went on to Jerusalem where he would be crucified, because that's what he had come to do for us. He knew that we needed him and his love, and that we wouldn't have it if he just stayed there on the mountain.

And that's why he doesn't want us just to share his love in the church, either. He doesn't want us just to stay in our box with it. After all, when we go outside the walls *(begin folding each side of the box down)* we discover that people need us; they need our love; they need our help; they need Jesus, and if we just stay here in our box *(fold up the sides again)* we won't be helping them, and we won't be sharing him.

Maybe that's why it's such a good thing to remind each other that Jesus came to take away our sin, and when he did that, he also folded down our walls *(indicate it with your action)* to send us out where people need us.

Why Not?

SCRIPTURE

And Jesus, full of the Holy Spirit, returned from the Jordan, and was led by the Spirit for forty days in the wilderness, tempted by the devil.

Luke 4:1 (First Sunday in Lent)

PREPARATION

You will need a report card if one is available, on which you can mark a set of A+ grades. (Most local schools will be willing to make one available. Otherwise it's a simple matter to produce a simulated one from cardboard.) You will also need a wrapper for a candy bar and a picture of a bicycle, and finally a picture of the crucifixion scene. (If none is available, look through the pictures in a church supply catalog and use one of the crucifixes shown. Otherwise a plain cross can be used, but it does not have quite the same effect.)

This morning I want to show you some things I have, and I'm really happy I have them. I wanted all of them very, very much, and I think you'll know why. Here is the first one. *(Show the report card.)* That's really a good report card, isn't it? And do you know something, I didn't think that I would get a report card like that, because I hadn't studied very much. But do you know what I did when the test came? I snuck in and looked at a copy of it on the teacher's desk, and then I looked up all the answers. That was really smart, wasn't it? *(Allow the children to comment. If one or two agree with you, don't worry about it. There will be enough who know it was cheating, and who will be glad to inform you of it.)* But . . . I wanted a good grade, and if I didn't cheat, how would I get it? *(Again, allow conversation. Undoubtedly someone will volunteer that you should have studied.)* Oh, sure, I could have studied, but think of all the work that would have been. It would have been so hard, and this was so easy . . . so why not?

Well, let me show you something else I'm happy about, since you don't feel so happy about how I got my good grades. This was from a candy bar I had yesterday. I was walking through a store and I wanted a candy bar, but I didn't have any money. But when no one was looking I just sort of sneaked this one. It didn't even cost me anything. How about that? Wasn't that neat? *(Permit comments again, leading children to tell that a person might earn the money somehow to buy the candy.)* But that would mean working, and working can be hard, and this was so easy. So, why not?

You still don't agree with me, do you? I don't even know whether to tell you about this one. Do you see this? It's my new bike. Of course, I don't even have it together yet. You see, last evening when all the people in the store were busy in the front, I saw this out in the back in a box, so I just pushed it around the corner, and then when no one was around I put it in my car, and that means it didn't cost me anything. *(Again, involve the children in conversation.)* But it was an easy way, so why not?

Now, I know that all of you know I was teasing you. I wouldn't cheat on a test or steal a candy bar or take a bicycle, even though those might seem like easy ways. But the easy way might not be the right way. Do you remember the Gospel lesson today, when the devil tried to get Jesus to take the easy way to get some bread or to get all the power in the world or even to prove that he was the son of God? Well, Jesus knew it was wrong, too, and he didn't do it; he didn't take the easy way. He took the way he had come to take, of suffering and dying for us. It was a hard way, but it was the only way. He didn't say "Why not?" He said, "Devil, you shouldn't try to make me sin." And do you know something? Because he said that, we can say it, too. We can say: "Devil, get away. Jesus is here with me." And to that, we can always say: "Why not?"

Don't Miss Out

SCRIPTURE

O Jerusalem, Jerusalem, killing the prophets and stoning those who are sent to you! How often would I have gathered your children together as a hen gathers her brood under her wings, and you would not! Behold, your house is forsaken. And I tell you, you will not see me until you say, "Blessed be he who comes in the name of the Lord!"

Luke 13:34-35 (Second Sunday in Lent)

PREPARATION

There is no special preparation needed for this message, since it is in the form of a story.

Sometimes instead of showing you something for our sermon together, I like to tell you something, or tell you about someone. And perhaps some of you remember a little boy we've talked about, whose name was Timmy. I don't know just how old he was, maybe about as old as _____ or _____ or _____. But that's not really important, anyway.

I want to tell you about a problem Timmy had. You might call it a problem with his ears, but it wasn't a problem an ear doctor could make better. It was a problem that often Timmy didn't want to listen when his mother called him. He'd rather play or ride his bike or read comics with his friends.

But one day, Timmy's uncle came to the house with some exciting news. He had come to surprise Timmy by taking him to the circus. So mother called Timmy. But when Timmy heard mother, he thought she might have an errand for him, so he just pedaled his bike away as fast as he could. His uncle waited and waited, but finally he couldn't wait any longer, and he went to the circus by himself. Just think of what Timmy missed!

40

Another day, Timmy was flying his kite in the park, when father came home early. He was going to take the family to a ball game, but when Timmy's big brother, Denny, came to tell Tim, Timmy wouldn't believe him. So father took the rest of the family, but Timmy came home to a baby sitter. He'd missed out again.

But one of the saddest things happened when grandmother and grandfather came to visit. They hadn't seen Timmy for so long, they really wanted to see him. But once again, Timmy pretended he didn't hear mother calling, and just kept on watching TV with another friend. He missed out on something again.

Those are not funny stories, are they? Not at all; they're sad stories. But do you know, they are not nearly as sad as a story about us and some of the things we miss out on. You see, Jesus comes to us with his words of love and forgiveness, but sometimes we stay home from church or Sunday school and don't even hear them. We know he is calling us, but we do our other things. He comes to us in his body and blood in Holy Communion, but we say, "Not right now" and we miss out on that, too, because we have our other things to do. He tells us we can pray to him, but we don't have time. We can read about him, but we don't have time for that either. We're just like Timmy with his uncle or his father or his grandparents; we don't want to hear, and then we miss out. We miss out on his love and his forgiveness; we miss out on the good news of all he has done for us.

But do you know something? Jesus still calls us, anyway. He loves us so much that he is still always here with us, waiting for us. He forgives us all our excuses and all our poor hearing, and gives us a new life where we don't have to miss out on anything.

The God Who Tries Again

SCRIPTURE

And he told this parable: "A man had a fig tree planted in his vineyard; and he came seeking fruit on it and found none. And he said to the vinedresser. 'Lo, these three years I have come seeking fruit on this fig tree, and I find none. Cut it down; why should it use up the ground?' And he answered him, 'Let it alone, sir, this year also, till I dig about it and put on manure. And if it bears fruit next year, well and good; but if not, you can cut it down.' "

Luke 13:6-9 (Third Sunday in Lent)

PREPARATION

There are several possible approaches to this particular message. The first would be using a guitar, which has been mistuned completely, so that the first sounds are obviously out of tune. If the presenter can tune the guitar, fine; otherwise it will also be necessary to have a guitarist assist.

Or, the same thoughts can be presented using a flashlight in which neither the bulb nor the batteries work at the beginning. The message offered below used the guitar; if the flashlight is used, instead of tuning various strings, substituting a new bulb and then trying the light, substtuting one battery and trying, and finally substituting both batteries, with the point finally that if the switch stays off, there will still be no light.

Good morning. Today we're going to do something different. We're not going to have your sermon the way we usually do. Instead we're going to sing a song, and I have asked _____ to help us with his guitar. So, as soon as he gives us a tone, we'll sing "Jesus Loves Me, This I Know." So, _____, give us a tone, please. *(Wait until he strikes the chord, and then show your displeasure at the sound you heard.)* _____, is something wrong? That didn't sound very good at all! Why don't you throw that guitar out and get a new one? *(Have your guitarist instructed to answer something like, "Well, can't I try just one more time to make it sound better?" while he tunes one string with another.)* Are you ready now? O.K., let's try it again. Give us the tone, please. *(Again, go through the same process as before. If it happens the children are a bit amused don't worry about it; you'll be able to capitalize on it.)* Wow, that was still a bad sound; we're even laughing about it, _____. Why not get a different guitar? *(Again, let him answer: "I like this guitar, and maybe we can still make it sound good.")* All right, let's try it again. *(Repeat the process above one more time, until the guitar is in tune.)* There, that sounds better. Now it sounds like a guitar is supposed to sound. I'm glad you were so patient. Otherwise your guitar might have ended up in the trash.

(Turning to children.) But do you know something? His guitar is something like we are. God would like us to make the good sounds of his love to him, to our parents and our relatives, and to each other. Sometimes we don't. We make angry sounds or disobedient sounds. Instead of sounds of praying, we hear bad words; even instead of people happy to sing, we hear grumpy sounds. If God would be impatient with us, he'd throw us on the scrap heap, just like I wanted to do with this guitar. But _____ likes his guitar, and so he was very patient with it, and God not only likes us, he loves us, and so he is patient with us, too. He shares his word with us, to tune us up. He sent Jesus into the world to take all the bad sounds from us. He's a God who just keeps trying again and again and again.

And because he does, we have a reason to sing, so let's do it.

(Lead the children in one stanza of "Jesus Loves Me" with the guitar accompanying. You might even invite the congregation to join in the chorus.)

The Dirty Doll

SCRIPTURE

Now the tax collectors and sinners were all drawing near to him. And the Pharisees and the scribes murmured, saying, "This man receives sinners and eats with them."

But the father said to his servants, "Bring quickly the best robe, and put it on him; and put a ring on his hand, and shoes on his feet; and bring the fatted calf and kill it, and let us eat and make merry; for this my son was dead, and is alive again, he was lost, and is found." And they began to make merry.

Luke 15:1-3, 22-24 (Fourth Sunday in Lent)

PREPARATION

You will need a child's doll, with one set of clothes which you can soil, and another set of clothes to replace them. (NOTE: If possible, borrow this doll from one of the families, *without* the child knowing that you have it. Instruct the family member you contact to permit the child to think the doll has been lost.)

This morning I am going to show you something that many of you will recognize, but one person especially will know. *(During this time, hold the doll behind your back.)* That one person is Sheryl, and she'll know what I have, I'm sure. *(Show the doll.)* Do you recognize this, Sheryl? *(Wait for response.)* What did you think had happened to it? *(Engage her in some conversation, leading to the point that she probably felt her doll was lost and she would never see it again.)* How do you feel now that you know your doll is safe, and that I just borrowed it to use today?

But let's look at this doll. Actually, it's not in such good shape anymore. It looks dirty, doesn't it? *(If the doll is a washable doll, have some dirt smears on the face and arms.)* And look at these clothes; they're dirty, too. What

44

do you think we can do about that? *(Again, let the children participate in discussion, leading them to the idea that "We'll clean the doll.")* That's right; we'll get the doll all cleaned up again. *(If the circumstances permit, have a small bowl with water and a cloth to clean the dirt.)* There! Now her face and hands are clean again! But what about these dirty old clothes? Maybe we should throw the doll away since her clothes are dirty. Do you agree, Sheryl, or would you rather put some clean clothes on her?

Sheryl, you might like to have these. *(Indicate the clean clothes you have.)* What are they? Of course; they're clean clothes for your doll. Would you like to put them on her? *(As Sheryl does, continue.)*

Do you know, we have something here just like a story Jesus told, about a young man who went away from home. His father thought he was lost. But when the young man came back, the father was so happy to see him that he brought out a new ring and new clothes and had a party. He was just as surprised as Sheryl was to find her doll again; probably he was even more surprised and happy, since people are more important than dolls. But, Sheryl, are you happy to have your doll back?

You see, Jesus was telling us that he is like that, too. We don't always do just the things he wants us to do; we sort of run away from him, and that's almost like being lost. But then he finds us again with his love for us. He washes away the dirt of our sins, and gives us not new clothes like these *(indicate your own clothes)* but the new clothes of his forgiveness. But how do you think Sheryl felt when she found her doll again? And how do you think the man felt when his son came home again? And so how do you think Jesus feels when we come to him? That's right; he's happy about it. And we can be happy too; we're not dirty dolls. We're his children!

How Would You Play The Game?

SCRIPTURE

And he began to tell the people this parable: "A man planted a vineyard, and let it out to tenants, and went into another country for a long while. When the time came, he sent a servant to the tenants, that they should give him some of the fruit of the vineyard; but the tenants beat him, and sent him away empty-handed. And he sent another servant; and him also they beat and treated shamefully, and sent him away empty-handed. And he sent yet a third; this one they wounded and cast out. Then the owner of the vineyard said, 'What shall I do? I will send my beloved son; it may be that they will respect him.' But when the tenants saw him, they said to themselves, 'This is the heir; let us kill him, that the inheritance may be ours.' And they cast him out of the vineyard and killed him. What then will the owner of the vineyard do to them? He will come and destroy those tenants, and give the vineyard to others." When they heard this, they said, "God forbid!" But he looked at them and said, "What then is this that is written:

'The very stone which the builders rejected
has become the head of the corner'?
Every one who falls on that stone will be broken to pieces; but when it falls on any one it will crush him."

Luke 20:9-18 (Fifth Sunday in Lent)

PREPARATION

You will need someone chosen beforehand to assist you with this presentation. (Necessary instructions will be clear from reading the message.) You will also need a ball of some kind, depending on the season and the sport you wish to use as your model.

This morning we're really going to do something different. We're going to pretend we're playing baseball. How about that? It's a game we all like, I know. But while I explain a couple things about how we're going to do it, I'm going to ask John to hold the ball for me. *(Give him the ball, and then give some instructions to several of the others about where to stand, and so forth. This need not be a long process.)*

All right, John, I'd like to have the ball now, if you please, so will you give it to Debbie? Then she can toss it to Rick, and we'll be playing. *(John refuses to give the ball to Debbie.)* Well, we have a problem, don't we? John won't give the ball to Debbie, and that means we can't play. Perhaps he'll give it to someone else. Rick, why don't you get it from John? *(Again, John refuses.)* Something is really wrong here, isn't it? But we'll try once more. Amy, you get the ball from John; maybe he'll give it to you. *(This time John not only refuses to give the ball back, but he also pushes Amy away.)*

Now, John, that wasn't very nice. I guess I'll have to take the ball away from you. I wanted you to play with us. But you really have treated us all badly. So you won't get to play any longer. *(Take the ball from him; he might resist for a second or so, but then give it back.)*

That was really sad, wasn't it? John just wanted everything his way, and when we wanted him to play our way, he wouldn't do it, and now he doesn't get to play at all.

But do you know something? That's the way we do with God sometimes. He gave us his word in the Bible, and he sent Jesus to us. But we still like to have our own way about everything; we don't even like to hear it when God tells us that we might be wrong about things. We might even say that we don't "play ball" with God.

So we really couldn't blame God if he decided to take his word away from us, could we? But the good news is that he doesn't! He did send Jesus to take away all our sins, that sin too, and he continues to love us and forgive us, hoping that we'll do things his way. And that's not just playing a game; that's living our life.

Oh, yes, one thing more. John really isn't that disobedient; I told him beforehand how I wanted him to act.

Our New Sound

SCRIPTURE

As he was now drawing near, at the descent of the Mount of Olives, the whole multitude of the disciples began to rejoice and praise God with a loud voice for all the mighty works that they had seen, saying, "Blessed be the King, who comes in the name of the Lord! Peace in heaven and glory in the highest!" And some of the Pharisees in the multitude said to him, "Teacher, rebuke your the very stones would cry out."
disciples." He answered, "I tell you, if these were silent,

Luke 19:37-40 (Sunday of the Passion—Palm Sunday)

PREPARATION

Prepare three sets of flash cards, all of the same size, preferably at least 4 x 8 inches, with three cards in each set. Each set will have the same word on all three cards, but the first one will be printed in very small letters, the second one in large letters, and the third one in still larger letters.

Set # 1 will have the word "Help!" on all three cards.
Set # 2 will have the word "Hurrah!"
Set # 3 will have the word "Hosanna!"

This morning I'm going to ask you to help me, by reading some words for me, and I'd like you to read the words the way you think these cards tell you to read them. Let's look at this set. *(Show the first set, with the smallest print first.)* Do you see these three cards? Now let's then say the words the way the card seems to say it. Here's the first one *(show the first card with the small print)* and that would seem to be small sound, wouldn't it? Let's say it that way. Very good! Now let's say it this way. *(Show the second card.)* Fine; that was a little louder. Now let's hear it this way. *(Show the last card.)* Very good! You really sounded like you meant it. Now, just one question. Suppose that you were swimming in a lake and got your feet stuck in the mud; how would you say this word then?

(Show the word again.) Of course you would; you really would mean that.

Well, let's look at another card. *(Show the second.)* Let's say this one the way each card tells us to say it. *(Repeat the action as with the first card.)* Now, suppose your team was losing the baseball game, but in the last inning one of your friends hit a home run with two people on base and you won the game. How would you say this word then?

Now let's look at our third word. This is a little different word, because it's one we don't say all the time. In fact, we hardly ever say it; I wonder if anyone knows what it means. *(Wait for response.)* Actually, it means "Save us, Lord!" and it's like saying "Hurrah!" and "Help!" at the same time. It's a way of saying hello to Jesus, welcoming him and telling him we need his help. Now, which card do you think I should hold up so we can say "Hosanna?" *(The children will indicate the one with the larger letters, so hold it up for them until they say the word.)* Very good! That's the way our welcome to Jesus should sound.

It's sad though, that sometimes our greeting to Jesus doesn't sound that way at all. Sometimes it's like this *(show the first card)* and sometimes like this. *(Show the second.)* Maybe we're too tired or too bored or have too many other thoughts or something. But maybe that's just when we really ought to say it like this. *(Show the larger card.)*

Or perhaps that's when we ought to say this. *(Show the "Help" card with the largest letters.)* And because Jesus does come to help us with his forgiveness, we can say this. *(Show the "Hurrah" card with the largest letters, and wait for the response.)* I know; let's put them together by saying this. *(Show the "Hosanna" cards, starting with the smallest, then the second one, and finally the largest letters.)* Great! That was a good sound. It's really a new sound for us all the time.

A Time to Be Happy

SCRIPTURE

But on the first day of the week, at early dawn, they went to the tomb, taking the spices which they had prepared. And they found the stone rolled away from the tomb, but when they went in they did not find the body. While they were perplexed about this, behold, two men stood by them in dazzling apparel; and as they were frightened and bowed their faces to the ground, the men said to them, "Why do you seek the living among the dead? Remember how he told you, while he was still in Galilee, that the Son of man must be delivered into the hands of sinful men, and be crucified, and on the third day rise."

Luke 24:1-8 (Easter Day)

PREPARATION

You will need a box, with a cover, which can be lined with white paper. You may wish to add a few lines of yellow marker paint or yellow Day-Glo lines to the white paper, to symbolize the brightness which the presence of the angels suggests. The cover is to represent the rock in front of the grave, so this will be held toward the children in the presentation.

This is really a happy day, isn't it? I wonder who can tell me what makes today so special. *(Wait for response, and then develop the idea in a few more questions or sentences.)* That's right; today is Easter day, the day that Jesus came out of the grave.

So today, I want you to help me tell the story about Jesus by showing me with your faces how you would feel about everything. We're going to pretend that this box is Jesus' grave, and we're going to pretend that we're his friends going there. So first of all, show me how you would feel when you think about Jesus having died. *(Indicate with your own expression.)* That's right; we'd all feel sad, wouldn't we? Just think, our friend has died and we won't see him again. That would make us sad.

Now show me how you would be feeling when you went to the grave to put some perfume on Jesus. *(Again, wait; you may wish to pick out one or two children to ask about the reason for their sad faces.)* That's right; you would still be sad, wouldn't you? *(During this time you will be holding the box in front of the children, with the cover closed.)*

How would you feel when you came to the grave and saw that the door was open? I think we'd be surprised, wouldn't we? How can we show that? *(Actually, the children will probably be better able to do it than most adults, so don't hesitate in letting them show the way.)*

But then comes the biggest surprise of all. *(Open the box.)* Not only is the door open, but Jesus is gone, and the angels tell you that he is alive again. Now, how do you feel? *(Wait again.)* That's right; we'd be really happy, wouldn't we? Show me again! Today is a happy day. It was a happy day for Jesus' disciples who thought their friend was dead, but then found out he was alive and would be with them again. Show me once more how that would make you feel if you were one of them.

But do you know, there's even more good news for us. Because of Jesus, we have more reason to be happy. We'll die too, someday. Show me how you feel when you think about that. *(Demonstrate with your own sad face.)* That's right; that would make us sad. But, because Jesus rose from his grave, he's going to wake us up out of ours, and they'll be just as empty as his. *(Demonstrate with the box.)* How do you feel about that? *(Wait for the happy expressions.)* Of course, that's the way we'll be. And just think; it's all because of today. So have a happy Easter! And show everybody about it!

Any Questions?

SCRIPTURE

Now Thomas, one of the twelve, called the Twin, was not with them when Jesus came. So the other disciples told him, "We have seen the Lord." But he said to them, "Unless I see in his hands the print of the nails, and place my finger in the mark of the nails, and place my hand in his side, I will not believe."

Eight days later, his disciples were again in the house, and Thomas was with them. The doors were shut, but Jesus came and stood among them, and said, "Peace be with you." Then he said to Thomas, "Put your finger here, and see my hands; and put out your hand, and place it in my side; do not be faithless, but believing." Thomas answered him, "My Lord and my God!" Jesus said to him, "Have you believed because you have seen me? Blessed are those who have not seen and yet believe."

John 20:24-29 (Second Sunday of Easter)

PREPARATION

Prepare three pieces of paper, each to have a large question mark in the center. You will also need a wastebasket and a box with a cover.

On the back side of the third paper print the words "JESUS LIVES!"

I wonder who can tell me what this mark means. *(Show the question mark.)* That's right; it's a question mark, and we use it to show that we are asking about something. Let me show you. Here's a question: How many of you like candy? *(Point to the question mark, and then make a show of counting the hands.)* Very good; you knew it was a question, and you also knew the answer. That was an easy one, wasn't it? *(Point to the question mark again.)* Do you see what this mark means? It means that we ask about things, and we get answers.

But sometimes it doesn't work out that way, especially

when our questions are about things we think we really ought to know. Maybe we have a question about something Jesus said, and we're afraid people will laugh if we ask it. *(As you are saying this, hold up the question mark.)* We're so afraid that we don't ask the question at all; instead we just sort of put it aside *(crumple up the paper and toss it in the wastebasket)* and forget all about it. Or perhaps we think it's a question that no one can answer. *(Hold up another question mark.)* So again, we don't ask it; instead we just keep it in our minds, and think about it every now and then. *(Place the paper in the box.)* It's like putting it away in this box, and rarely thinking about it again. *(Act out the process, opening the box, taking out the question, scratching your head, placing the paper back in the box, etc.)*

The sad thing is that neither this way *(indicate the wastebasket)* nor this way *(indicate the box)* helps us at all. We still have our questions, but we don't have the answers. There is a better way.

The better way is the one Thomas shows us in our Gospel lesson today. He had some questions about Jesus and his resurrection; he didn't even know if he could believe it. But instead of putting that question out of his mind *(show the wastebasket)* or covering it up without asking *(show the box)* he said it out loud. *(Show the third paper.)* And then he found his answer. *(Reverse the paper to show the words "Jesus lives!")* But that's an answer he wouldn't have known if he hadn't asked his questions.

And that's the Good News we have today. Jesus does live, just as we heard on Easter Sunday. And because he does, we don't have to be afraid to ask about him. We don't have to laugh at others when they ask questions, or cover up our questions because we're afraid they'll laugh at us. We can ask the questions we want to ask *(show the question mark)* because *(reverse the paper and wait for the children to read)* Jesus lives! Any questions?

We Know Him Too

SCRIPTURE

When they got out on land, they saw a charcoal fire there, with fish lying on it, and bread. Jesus said to them, "Bring some of the fish that you have just caught." So Simon Peter went aboard and hauled the net ashore, full of large fish, a hundred and fifty-three of them; and although there were so many, the net was not torn. Jesus said to them, "Come and have breakfast." Now none of the disciples dared ask him, "Who are you?" They knew it was the Lord.

John 21:9-12 (Third Sunday of Easter)

PREPARATION

Necessary for this message are a baseball and glove, a guitar, a fishing reel or lure, a cross, a communion wafer, and a small Bible.

This morning I'm going to ask all of you to help me again, by looking at some things and answering some questions for me. First of all, this. *(Show the baseball and glove.)* What kind of person would use this? *(Wait for the answers.)* That's right; these are for a ball player, and as soon as we see someone with these, we can be sure that he plays ball. How about this? *(Show the guitar.)* That's right; this person would be a musician. A guitar is a musical instrument, and so the person playing one would be a musician, right? *(Nod your head. You will notice the involved children responding by nodding also.)* And what about this? *(Show the reel or the lure.)* Who would use this? Of course; this is something a fisherman would use. And it's true, isn't it, that we would recognize the people by these things. We recognize a ball player *(show the equipment)* or a musician *(show the guitar)* or a fisherman. *(Show the reel or the lure.)*

But sometimes it's not quite that easy. I have some other

things to show you, and we'll see who we recognize from them. First of all, what is this? *(Show the cross, and wait for response.)* Or, what is this? *(Show the communion wafer, and wait again.)* How about this? *(Show the Bible.)* Very good! We could all recognize these things easily. But just recognizing the things isn't quite all we really want to do. There's something more important for us. Just as we recognized people through these things *(indicate the first items you showed)* so we can recognize a special person through these. Let's just think a minute; who made the cross something special for everyone? How did he do that? *(Wait for response, leading to the fact that Jesus died on it.)* But is he still dead? *(Again wait for response, leading to the idea that on Easter he rose.)* That's right; this cross reminds us of Jesus. He died on one, and on Easter he rose; that's why this cross is empty. He isn't on it any more. And now we're ready to look at something else.

(Show the wafer.) Because of this *(show the cross)* we can recognize Jesus in this. *(Show the wafer again.)* When we receive Holy Communion, he is coming to us to show us how much he loves us. And here's another way we can recognize him. *(Show the Bible.)* This is the way he comes to us too. He gives us his love and his forgiveness through this too.

That means we're almost like his first people. This morning in the Gospel lesson you heard how they recognized him when he did a miracle and had them catch a hundred fifty-three fish all at once, and then they knew him for sure when he showed his love to them by making breakfast for them. This is our miracle *(show the cross)* and this is the way he is still showing his love to us. *(Show the wafer and the Bible.)* The disciples knew him that way, and just think, we know him, too.

Hearing His Voice

SCRIPTURE

My sheep hear my voice, and I know them, and they follow me; and I give them eternal life, and they shall never perish, and no one shall snatch them out of my hand.

John 10:27-28 (Fourth Sunday of Easter)

PREPARATION

Some advance preparation is necessary for this presentation, involving one or two parents from the congregation whose children participate in the children's sermons. Tape record their voices, with these instructions to be recorded:

"Lisa, you know who this is. I'd like you to hold up your hand." (To be recorded by Lisa's father.)

"Lisa, you heard your father; please do it now." (That to be recorded by the mother.)

If you are using two sets of parents for the recording, you might have the second set say something like this:

"Timmy, this is Mother. Would you fold your hands, please?" and

"Tim, you know who this is; did you do what Mother asked?"

You will also need a pillow or blanket to use in covering up the recorder, muffling the sound.

All of you know what this is, don't you? *(Show the recorder, and permit the children to respond to your question.)* Well, let's see what we have recorded on it. *(Play the first statements by the first set of parents, and while you continue talking, reverse the recorder to play them again.)* Now, what was that? Did anyone recognize the voices? Let's hear them again. This time, if there is someone here who recognizes the voices, I'd like that person to do what the voices say. *(Play the statements again. If necessary, help Lisa recognize her parents' voices, or at least acknowledge that she did.)* Did you know those voices, Lisa? How? That's right! Those were your father and mother speaking. And did you do what they told you to do? Of course; you knew their voices and you did what they wanted. Very good!

Now let's listen again. *(Play the second set, involving the person in the same way.)* Did you know those voices, Tim? Who were they? Of course; those voices belonged to your parents. And you did the same thing Lisa did, didn't you? You knew the voices and did what they asked.

But now, let's try it again, a different way. *(Cover up the recorder with the blanket or pillow to muffle the sound.)* Let's listen, now. *(Demonstrate the muffled sound.)* That makes it very difficult, doesn't it? I really couldn't even recognize the voices at all. And it's very hard to follow someone's instructions when we don't recognize what they're saying, isn't it?

And do you know, that's the way it is with God's people and Jesus too. He speaks to us in his special way through his word, and we recognize his voice and do the things he likes us to do, at least as much as we can. But sometimes we let things get in the way and his voice is all muffled. *(Indicate the pillow and the recorder.)* We just don't hear him too well. Maybe our mind is on other things *(wrap the pillow a bit tighter)* or maybe we just don't want to listen to him *(tighten the pillow a little more)* or perhaps we're too tired or too restless or something like that. Sometimes we even turn him off all the way. *(Turn off the recorder.)* And then we can't hear his voice at all.

But that's why Jesus came to the world. He wanted us to follow him. So he took away all the sins that get in the way of hearing his voice and recognizing it. *(Unwrap the recorder.)* He comes to us in his word and his sacrament to "turn us on" again as his people. *(Turn on the recorder.)* Just think, when we take these things away *(indicate the blanket or pillow you have used)* we can hear this *(indicate recorder)* better. And when Jesus took our sins away, it meant that we can hear him again. We are his people, hearing his voice.

The Important Thing

SCRIPTURE

When he had gone out, Jesus said, "Now is the Son of man glorified, and in him God is glorified; if God is glorified in him, God will also glorify him in himself, and glorify him at once. Little children, yet a little while I am with you. You will seek me; and as I said to the Jews so now I say to you, 'Where I am going you cannot come.' A new commandment I give to you, that you love one another; even as I have loved you, that you also love one another. By this all men will know that you are my disciples, if you have love for one another."

John 13:31-35 (Fifth Sunday of Easter)

PREPARATION

Prepare a set of flash cards approximately 3 x 6 inches each, as follows:

We have a beautiful church.
Our pews are comfortable.
We have new clothes.
We help poor people.
We have a good choir.
Our church has many people.
We love each other.
Our hymn books are pretty.

This morning I'm really going to need your help in making some very important decisions. I have a set of flash cards which tells us something about the church here. Now, of course, we know that the church is really people. So what we're going to be deciding is how important different things are for God's people, his church. Let's see, how will we decide? *(Pretend to be thinking about the process.)* I've got it; we'll look at each card and decide if it's very important, sort of important, or not important at all. Does everybody understand that? O.K.?

Here's the first one. Let's read it together. "We have a beautiful church." Well, how about that? Our church building is beautiful, isn't it? People really showed that they love God when they gave the money to build this fine building. That's pretty important, isn't it? *(Allow the children to react and to discuss. DON'T BE AFRAID TO INVOLVE THEM IN THE PROCESS OF THIS DECISION MAKING. You will be surprised at the quality of their answers and at the simultaneous involvement of the congregation, as well.)* Well, let's put it on this stack for the things that are sort of important, agree? *(Continue with the other cards, allowing the children to decide how they rate the various items, commenting as you choose, perhaps trying to talk them out of some of their ideas. This is meant to be a relaxed, communicating experience; allow it to be so.)*

Now let's see. These are the things that all of us like, I am sure, but we really say that they're not the most important thing in the church. And here are some others *(indicate the middle group)* which are a little more important; we like the things they talk about, too. But here are the most important things; we love each other and we help the poor. Of all our cards, these are the most important.

Do you know something? That's exactly what Jesus said. He said that people will know that we are his disciples if we love one another. That's the most important thing to be doing. But the sad thing is that it's easy to get mixed up. We look at things like clothes and buildings and comfortable chairs and make those the most important. We get the stacks switched around sometimes.

But that's why Jesus came to the world. He didn't want us to be all caught up in switched around lives. With his forgiveness he opens our eyes to the right things and the most important things; with his love he gives us the power to love. *(Show the cards of loving and helping the poor.)* Those are the things that were most important to him, and those are the things most important to us, when we follow him. That's the good news we have this morning; with Jesus we're back in the right direction, living for the important things.

59

Keeping His Word

SCRIPTURE

Jesus answered him, "If a man loves me, he will keep my word, and my Father will love him, and we will come to him, and make our home with him. He who does not love me does not keep my words; and the word which you hear is not mine but the Father's who sent me."

John 14:23-24 (Sixth Sunday of Easter)

PREPARATION

You will need several Bibles for this message. One of them should fit into a box which can be closed; another should be of rough leather, so that dust will show on it. A third should open up to show a heart folded into it.

You will also need a flash card with the words "LOVE YOUR NEIGHBOR" written or printed on it, and a large heart with the words "helping," "sharing," "giving," and "caring" printed in a column in the center.

Did you hear the Gospel lesson in church this morning? I wonder if you remember when we read about Jesus saying these words: "If a man loves me, he will keep my word." That's what Jesus said, isn't it? So, I wonder, how many of us love Jesus? *(Wait for response.)* Very good! We all do, don't we? So what does that mean we will do? Jesus said, "If a man loves me, he will keep my word." What will we do? *(Wait again.)* That's right; we will keep his word.

This morning we're going to look at some ways people keep his word. What is this? That's right; it's a Bible, and we all know the Bible is the record of some of the words of Jesus. So, perhaps we can keep his word by putting it away, where we can keep it hidden. Do you think that's what Jesus meant? *(Involve the children in the discussion; allow them to answer also why they do not think Jesus meant keeping it that way.)* Right! That's more like keeping the word away than like keeping it, isn't it?

How about this way of keeping the word? *(Show the dusty Bible.)* I keep this on the coffee table in the living room, so people can see it. Of course, I don't use it much; that's why it's so dusty. *(Dust the cover.)* But I'm keeping the word where people can see it. Maybe that's what Jesus meant. Do you think so? *(Again, engage the children in conversation.)*

Well, how about this one? *(Show the flash card.)* This is a word from Jesus, and it's an easy one to remember. In fact, let's memorize it together. Love your neighbor. Now let's all say it. *(Have the children repeat it.)* Very good! We've learned that word of Jesus. Now we have it in our minds and we can keep it there. How about that? We've memorized the word of Jesus; is that keeping it? *(Again, permit some response, leading to the thought that just memorizing isn't keeping the word.)*

That's really something, isn't it? We've found some different things people do with the word, and think they're keeping it, but we've found out that none of them are really keeping the word at all. So how about this? *(Show the heart, holding it reversed to the children so that they cannot see the words you have printed on it.)* This means love, doesn't it? Now let's look at some of the ways we can show love. *(Have the children read the words.)* What do you say about that? If we do these things, are we keeping the word? Of course we are, and that's the way Jesus meant for us to keep it.

(Show the third Bible, with the heart in it.) You see, that's what this book is all about. *(Open to show the heart.)* It's about the love God has for us. But he didn't keep that love hidden away, or let it collect dust, or just say words about it. He sent Jesus to help and love and share and care, to suffer and die to take our sins away. He gives us his love *(show the heart again)* so that we can give it to others. *(Show the heart with the action words on it.)* And when God's people do this, we're keeping his word.

We're Together!

SCRIPTURE

"I do not pray for these only, but also for those who are to believe in me through their word, that they may all be one; even as thou, Father, art in me, and I in thee, that they also may be in us, so that the world may believe that thou hast sent me. The glory which thou hast given me I have given to them, that they may be one even as we are one, I in them and thou in me, so that the world may know that thou hast sent me and hast loved them even as thou hast loved me."

John 17:20-23 (Seventh Sunday of Easter)

PREPARATION

From heavy cardboard, cut a large numeral "1" at least twelve to fifteen inches high. Then cut this numeral into pieces, as if you were making a jig-saw puzzle out of it. On the pieces write the following:

I don't like some of the people there.

They sing the hymns too fast.

The sermons are too long.

I don't agree with the Sunday school superintendent.

They use a different translation of the Bible.

Arrange the pieces together on another piece of cardboard or light board to form the number. (You may wish to place a small circle of masking tape on the board to stick to both the board and the cardboard piece.)

This morning we're going to do a little mathematics exercise! How about that? You thought you were coming to church, but you're going to some numbers, instead. But don't be worried about it, even if you're not good at math; all we're going to do is look at one number and see who knows it. *(Show the board.)* Hold up your hand if you know the number, please. *(Wait for the hands to go up, and then call on one of the smaller children old enough to recognize the number.)* Very good! That's the number one, and it's not so hard after all, is it?

Perhaps we should say that recognizing a number one

isn't hard, but sometimes that number has something hard about it. You see, Jesus said that we are to be one with each other. That means that we're to be such close friends and so loving that we're sort of brought together with each other. When we help each other, we're being one with each other, or when we sing together, or when we pray together. Can anyone think of more ways we might be one with each other? *(Allow time for answer and discussion.)* Very good! When we're doing those things, we're being "one" just as Jesus prayed that we would be.

But sometimes, even in God's people, we have a hard time being one with each other. *(Read the various lines you have written, and as you do, take each piece from the number on the board.)* Do you see what is happening? When each person thinks of others, as we said before, then we can be one. But when we think of ourselves more than others *(indicate the stack of pieces)* we break everything up. Then we aren't one, anymore.

But that's why Jesus came to the world. He wanted his people to be one with him and one with each other. So he found the way to make them one. He did it by suffering and dying on his cross, to take away all their sins . . . no, all our sins . . . even our sins of thinking of ourselves so much of the time. He comes to us in his word and in the sacrament and brings us back to himself, and guess what, he brings us back to each other, too. That really makes us different, so different that we can say things like, "I'm really learning to like the people there." *(Place that piece back on the board.)* "It doesn't really matter if the hymns are a little faster than I like; others like them that way." *(Replace that piece.)*

(Continue with each piece of the puzzle until the numeral is complete again.) There! It's all back together again! Jesus is making us one, and the Good News we have is that we're together with him and together with each other. He prayed for it, and it can happen right here, with us. *(Show the number once more.)*

Candles, Cake, and Celebration

SCRIPTURE

"But when the Counselor comes, whom I shall send to you from the Father, even the Spirit of truth, who proceeds from the Father, he will bear witness to me; and you also are my witnesses, because you have been with me from the beginning.

"I did not say these things to you from the beginning, because I was with you. But now I am going to him who sent me; yet none of you asks me, 'Where are you going?' But because I have said these things to you, sorrow has filled your hearts. Nevertheless I tell you the truth: it is to your advantage that I go away, for if I do not go away, the Counselor will not come to you. And when he comes, he will convince the world concerning sin and righteousness and judgment: concerning sin, because they do not believe in me; concerning righteousness, because I go to the Father, and you will see me no more; concerning judgment, because the ruler of this world is judged."

John 15:26-27; 16:4b-11 (The Day of Pentecost)

PREPARATION

Using something like a round carton of the type in which cottage cheese is often packed, prepare a simulated birthday cake, either by coloring or by covering it with construction paper or even papier mache. (If possible, let the supposed frosting or covering be red, for the color of the Spirit.)

Cover three short pencils with construction paper, to serve as candles. On one candle print "forgiveness"; on another, the word "truth"; and on the third the words "a better way to live." These candles should be on the cake, but placed there in such a way they can be removed, and then later replaced.

I wonder who knows what I have this morning. *(Show the cake.)* That's right; it's a cake. But what kind of cake is it? Of course; it's a birthday cake. How did you know?

(Wait for answers.) But now let's ask something else. Why are we having a birthday cake today? *(Allow the children to answer. Even their wrong answers will help prepare the way for the answer you will give if none of them do.)* Would you like to know the real reason? It's because today is the birthday for the church! It's the day the church really started, when Jesus sent his Holy Spirit to the people, just as he said he would. And that's why we have a cake to celebrate it. The people knew something strange and good was happening to them when that new power came to them. And so we remember it and celebrate it, just like a birthday at home.

It's really a day for us to celebrate, too, because something strange and good is still happening to us. When we hear the Word of God or receive Jesus' body and blood in the sacrament, the Spirit is still coming to us, doing for us just what he did for the first Christians. That's why we have these candles today. They're the birthday candles for the church. Let's see what they say. *(Have the children read them together.)* That's right; those are the things that happen to us when the Holy Spirit comes. He leads us to the truth; he lets us know that we're forgiven people; he gives us new power for a new way to live.

Of course, it's sad that sometimes we don't really want to celebrate the birthday of the church or the power of the Spirit that way. Sometimes we insist on having our own ideas about things rather than God's *(remove the truth candle)* or we don't care about forgiveness *(remove that candle)* or we don't want to even try to change the bad things we do so that we have a better way to live. *(Remove that candle, too.)* Then it's a sad time instead of a celebrating time, though. And it's not much of a birthday cake without candles, is it?

But Jesus sends his Spirit to us. He leads us to the truth; he gives us his forgiveness, and in him we do have a better way to live. And that puts the candles back on our cake. *(Replace them, one by one.)*

Someone to Guide Us

SCRIPTURE

"When the Spirit of truth comes, he will guide you into all the truth."

John 16:13 (The Holy Trinity, The First Sunday after Pentecost)

PREPARATION

On one side of a board about three feet long, attach two narrow wood strips (heavy cardboard can also be used) to serve as guide rails for a small toy car to run between. The other side of the board will be left plain.

This morning I'm going to need someone to help me. Who would like to? *(Choose one of the children.)* Very good; Heidi will be my helper. So, Heidi, I'm going to give you this car *(show the toy)* and you will put it at the top of this hill I'm going to make with my board. *(Indicate by holding the board at a slant to make the hill. The guide rails should be hidden from view, with the plain side showing.)* So, Heidi, will you please place the car at the top of the hill and when I say "Go," let the car run down the hill. Do you understand? Fine! Go! *(As the car gathers momentum, turn the board just enough so that it goes off the edge.)* Oh, oh! That's too bad; we had a crash. The car didn't make it to the bottom. Let's try it again. *(Repeat the process, with the car going off the other edge this time.)*

Well, let's try it another way. *(Turn the board over, showing the guide rails.)* Heidi, do you see these guide rails? Let's place the car right in the middle of those two rails. *(Wait while she does so.)* Very good. Go! Look at that! Our car went all the way to the bottom of the hill. It's a good car, after all. It just needed a guide, and our rails *(indicate them)* guided it perfectly.

And do you know, that's just the way we are! When we were baptized Jesus made us his children. That's sort of the top of the hill, where we all start out. *(Indicate it with the board.)* And he sends his Spirit to us to guide us so that we can live the way his children ought to live. *(Indicate the guide rails.)* But sadly, sometimes we just want to do things our own way. *(Turn the board over.)* We don't want to follow guides at all. And then we have the crashes that we call sin. *(Reenact the process with the car without the guide rails, leaving the car on the floor.)*

But that's why we have something so important to share this morning. To have crashed up cars is sad enough, but to have crashed up people is worse. But the good news we have is that Jesus didn't leave us that way. He came to the world to pick up all the people who had crashed without him *(pick up the car)* and to give them a new guide to follow. *(Turn the board over.)* That new guide is his Holy Spirit, just as Jesus said he would be. And just think, we have two kinds of good news. We have Jesus to pick us up, and the Holy Spirit to guide us. *(Conclude by allowing the car to roll all the way down the hill, between the guide rails.)* And we have them all the way to heaven.

Here's Proof

SCRIPTURE

When he was not far from the house, the centurion sent friends to him, saying to him, "Lord, do not trouble yourself, for I am not worthy to have you come under my roof; therefore I did not presume to come to you. But say the word, and let my servant be healed."

When Jesus heard this he marveled at him, and turned and said to the multitude that followed him, "I tell you, not even in Israel have I found such faith."

Luke 7:6-7, 9 (Second Sunday after Pentecost)

PREPARATION

You will need a letter in an envelope, addressed to Timmy; you will also need a cross and a Bible.

This morning we're going to hear a story about one of the friends I like to tell you about. Maybe some of you remember his name; it's Timmy. You do remember, I'm sure, that Timmy is a rather little boy, about six years old. Sometimes he's very good, and sometimes he's not so good. He's just about like everyone else, I suppose. But now to our story.

One day Timmy was riding his bicycle down the hill, when he fell off. He wasn't hurt, but his bicycle just kept going down the hill. On and on it went, over the curb and out into the street where a big truck hit it and broke it all apart. Just imagine how Timmy felt. Maybe you could show me with your faces. (*Wait for a short time while the children act out their feelings.*) That's right; it was a sad time, and Timmy was very unhappy for days and days.

But then the mailman came with this letter for Timmy. (*Open it and read it, or have one of the children read it.*) "Dear Timmy: We're sorry to hear about your bicycle being wrecked, but we're happy that you are safe. And we want you to know that we're sending you a new bicycle to replace your old one. Love, Grandma and Grandpa." How about that? Now how do you think Timmy felt? Of course! He was very happy, and every day he watched for the parcel truck until his bicycle came. He didn't have to cry any more about the old bike. He knew from the letter that he'd have another one, because he knew his grandparents would do what they said. *(Show the letter.)* This was enough proof for him; he could depend on them.

And do you know, we're just like Timmy, only in a different way. It's not a bicycle that's wrecked for us; it's our lives. They are wrecked by that thing we call sin, all those wrong things we do. And when we think of that, we'd have to feel even worse than Timmy and his bicycle. But we have someone who loves us even more than grandparents love their grandchildren. We have Jesus, and this *(indicate the Bible)* is the letter in which he tells us how much he does love us. He doesn't want our lives to be spoiled by sin, so he took our sins away. That's why he came to earth in the first place, and everything he did, all his teaching and his healing and all his miracles and especially his suffering and dying on the cross were to make our lives better again, to give us new lives in place of the old. If you want proof for that, like Timmy might have wanted, here it is. *(Show the cross.)* And here's the letter telling us all about it. *(Show the Bible.)* And we can even say that we can believe this *(indicate the Bible)* because we know the one who proved his love with this. *(Show the cross.)* And that's real proof!

God Visits His People

SCRIPTURE

Soon afterward he went to a city called Nain, and his disciples and a great crowd went with him. As he drew near to the gate of the city, behold, a man who had died was being carried out, the only son of his mother, and she was a widow; and a large crowd from the city was with her. And when the Lord saw her, he had compassion on her and said to her, "Do not weep." And he came and touched the bier, and the bearers stood still. And he said, "Young man, I say to you, arise." And the dead man sat up, and began to speak. And he gave him to his mother. Fear seized them all; and they glorified God, saying, "A great prophet has risen among us!" and "God has visited his people!" And this report concerning him spread through the whole of Judea and all the surrounding country.

Luke 7:11-17 (Third Sunday after Pentecost)

PREPARATION

Needed for this message are a symbol of baptism, either a baptismal shell, if this is used and would be recognized by the children, or a baptismal certificate perhaps, a copy of the Scriptures, a communion wafer, and a chalice.

Do any of you remember the Gospel lesson this morning? What was it all about? *(If children can respond, encourage them, gradually drawing the story from them.)* That's right; it was about a really great miracle Jesus did. Of course, all of his miracles are really great, but this one almost seemed like it was something very, very special. That young man had died, and Jesus made him alive again, just like he will make us all alive when he comes back for us. But do you remember what the people said? Let me read part of it to you again: "They glorified God, saying, 'A great prophet has risen among us!' and 'God has visited his people!' " They looked at what Jesus did, and they said "God has visited his people!"

And that's exactly what we can say, when we look at the great things Jesus has done for us. First of all, he did this. *(Show the baptismal shell.)* That was a miracle, wasn't it? Just think, when you were baptized, he made you his very own child. Of course, you were probably too young to say it, but you really might have said, "Jesus is visiting me!" Or look at this. *(Show the copy of the Bible.)* We read this or hear it, and Jesus does another miracle for us; he gives us his love through this. What could we say about that? We could say, "Jesus is visiting his people!"

And certainly we could say the same thing with this miracle. *(Show the wafer and the chalice.)* What are these? *(Wait for the response.)* That's right, these are from communion, when Jesus gives us his body and his blood, and with them his love and his strength. That's almost like making us alive again, too, isn't it? What could we say about that, do you suppose? *(Wait for the children to respond; undoubtedly someone will offer, "Jesus is visiting us!" or something similar.)* Right! Jesus is visiting his people!

And that's the good news we have today. There might be times that we will have problems or be unhappy, just like some of the people in today's Gospel. But then all we have to do is think about the great things Jesus has done for us, and we don't have to be worried or sad any longer. We know that Jesus is visiting his people!

Who Loves More?

SCRIPTURE

"Therefore I tell you, her sins, which are many, are forgiven, for she loved much; but he who is forgiven little, loves little."

Luke 7:47 (Fourth Sunday after Pentecost)

PREPARATION

Prepare the following small cards. (Since individual children will read them, the cards need not be large.)

1. Henry thought his uncle was very stingy.
2. Tommy borrowed ten cents from his uncle. When he wanted to pay his uncle back, the uncle said, "Forget it, Tommy. You can keep it as a present."
3. James borrowed a dollar from his uncle. When he wanted to pay his uncle back, the uncle said, "I know how hard you worked to save that dollar, and I know how much you want that new model plane. Get that instead!"
4. Billy doesn't think that he does anything wrong.
5. Don knows that he does some things wrong, but feels that everybody else does wrong things, too.
6. Tim knows that he does many wrong things, but is happy that God forgives him.

Who would like to read some cards for us this morning? *(Choose three, and give out the first three cards.)* All right; we're going to hear these three cards. They're all about some people, and we're going to have to decide whether these boys would be loving boys, super-loving boys, or not so loving boys. So, we'll all have to listen to the cards very carefully before we make our decisions. First, let's hear about Henry. *(Have that card read.)* Do you think that would be loving, super-loving, or not so loving? *(Allow some discussion; it will probably come out just as you wish it to. Otherwise, you might lead it to that point, or even permit it to be different. It is not difficult to improvise from the children's answers.)* I think I'd agree;

Henry doesn't sound like he would be very loving toward his uncle.

Now let's put that card here, and then we'll listen to the next one. *(Have the next card read, and repeat the process of decision making.)* Fine, we'll put that card here. *(Now, repeat with the last of the set of cards.)*

We did very well with those cards, didn't we? And just the way we decided things seems to tell us that when people have done something good for us, we find it easier to love them. Isn't that what our decisions mean?

Now let's try another set of cards. Who would like to read these? *(Choose three children, and have them read the cards, one at a time.)* Now we've heard all of those, so let's ask the same questions we did before with these cards. *(Indicate the first set.)* We'll listen to each card, and then decide whether that person would love God a whole lot, a super-whole lot, or maybe just sort of love him a little bit, maybe. *(Carry out the process in the same way you did the first set. NOTE: THE CARDS NEED NOT BE READ IN ORDER. IT MAKES THE PROCESS MORE INTERESTING IF THEY ARE NOT.)*

Do you know, both sets of cards almost say the same things? They tell us that we even love God more when we think he loves us more. If we don't think we need his forgiveness and his love, then we probably don't love him so much. If we know how much we need his forgiveness and how fully we have it, then we'll be more loving, too.

And that's why Jesus came. He came to show us our sins, with his teaching about how we're really supposed to be. But that's only part of it. He did that so we would know how much we need him and his forgiveness. He knew that's the way our love for him would grow, and he wanted all of us to be in this stack of cards, with the super-loving people. That's why he showed such great love to us in the first place, even dying on the cross for us. He wants us to be those who love more. And the good news is that we can be, because he first loved us.

Who Is Jesus?

SCRIPTURE

Now it happened that as he was praying alone the disciples were with him; and he asked them, "Who do the people say that I am?" And they answered, "John the Baptist; but others say, Elijah; and others, that one of the old prophets has risen. And he said to them, "But who do you say that I am?" And Peter answered, "The Christ of God." But he charged and commanded them to tell this to no one, saying, "The Son of man must suffer many things, and be rejected by the elders and chief priests and scribes, and be killed, and on the third day be raised."

Luke 9:18-22 (Fifth Sunday after Pentecost)

PREPARATION

Materials needed for this presentation are a make-believe report card, with two categories listed, one for "Loving God" and the other for "Loving People"; a ruler; and a cross.

If you were listening carefully to the Gospel this morning you heard Jesus ask his disciples a question: "Who do people say that I am?" That's quite a question! What do people say about Jesus? Who do they think he is?

Well, here's one answer to that question. *(Show the report card.)* Who knows what this is? *(Wait for the response.)* That's right. This is a report card. And let me ask you another question; who gives report cards? *(Wait again for the response.)* That's right; teachers give us report cards. They teach us something, and then they give report cards to show us if we have learned what they wanted us to learn. And that's one answer to the question of who Jesus is. People think of him as a very good teacher, teaching us how to love God and how to love each other. *(Show the report card again.)* And in some ways that's true; Jesus did that. But he did much more.

(Show the ruler.) Here's another idea of Jesus. What do I have here? *(Wait for the response again.)* That's

good; I have a ruler. And what do we use a ruler for? *(Wait for the children to answer. You will probably have two answers: "For measuring things." and "For making straight lines." If those responses do not come quickly, it is easily possible to lead the children to them.)* Very good! A ruler is for measuring and for making things straight. And many people feel that's why Jesus came. They feel he measures how much we love him, then straightens us out.

But really, Jesus came for something other than those reasons. Of course, he was a great teacher, and with his word, he still is. *(Show the report card.)* And he does tell us to measure ourselves and our love. *(Show the ruler.)* But really, he came for this. *(Show the cross.)*

That's right; he came because of a cross. He came to suffer and die on that cross, so that we could be his children again. He knew that we would never be able to love him perfectly. *(Indicate the report card.)* And he knew that we could never measure up to all the things God's people should do. *(Show the ruler.)* He knew that we needed his forgiveness more than anything else. That's why he came.

Of course, sometimes we don't really like that idea. We like to think that we would get good grades in loving him and in loving each other. *(Show the report card.)* We like to think that we do really measure up to everything he wants. *(Show the ruler.)* We'd like to think that we're good enough, that we don't really need anyone to die for us. Those are our sins of pride. But that's exactly why Jesus came this way. *(Show the cross again.)* He knew that we needed his forgiveness more than his good teaching, helpful though that good teaching is. He knew that the only power to help us measure up *(indicate the ruler)* was his love. So who is Jesus? He's not just a teacher or someone who measures his people to see if they're doing things just right; he's the Savior who died on a cross. *(Show the cross.)* And that's the good news we have, because that's the Jesus we have.

75

How Would You Show It?

SCRIPTURE

As they were going along the road, a man said to him, "I will follow you wherever you go." And Jesus said to him, "Foxes have holes, and birds of the air have nests, but the Son of man has nowhere to lay his head." To another he said, "Follow me." But he said, "Lord, let me first go and bury my father." But he said to him, "Leave the dead to bury their own dead; but as for you, go and proclaim the kingdom of God." Another said, "I will follow you, Lord; but let me first say farewell to those at my home." Jesus said to him, "No one who puts his hand to the plow and looks back is fit for the kingdom of God."

Luke 9:57-62 (Sixth Sunday after Pentecost)

PREPARATION

You will need four or five items which children in your audience might be expected to enjoy, plus a Bible and a cross. The items might be such things as a guitar, a baseball, a doll, a book, etc. Or you might choose to use pictures instead of the actual items. (The message following is built on use of the items, but the technique and the message would be the same either way.)

This morning we're going to look at some things we all enjoy, or at least most of us do. I suppose that some of you might like some of these things better than others, but we'll soon see about that. Actually, that's what I want you to do; I want you to look at these things I'm going to show you, and tell me which one is your favorite. So let's start by looking at all of the things at once. *(Show all the items, one after the other, with simple comments about them, but without asking for any decision regarding them at this time.)* These are all things we like, aren't they? But I wonder, don't we like some of them better than others?

Let's look at this one. *(Show the ball.)* How many of you like to play ball? *(Count the hands.)* At least ten of you like to play ball; very good. Now how about this? *(Show the doll.)* How many of you like to play with dolls? *(Again, count the hands.)* Now let's find out something else. How many of you would rather play ball than play with dolls? *(Wait for the hands to go up again, and count them.)* That's very close; it's almost even.

Let's go on with the other things. *(Repeat the process with the other items you have, but DO NOT include the Bible or the cross.)*

That really tells us something, doesn't it? We all have favorite things to do. Some of us like one thing, some of us like another. That's just the way we are. But now I have another question. How will you prove to me that you like baseball better than dolls? *(Wait for answers, until someone has offered the idea that they would play baseball instead, and you could watch them, or some similar thought.)* How could you show that you like guitars better than books? *(Again wait for answers, hoping to lead the response to the idea that a person does the things he likes best.)*

Now I have something else to show you. *(Show the Bible.)* How many of you know what this is? How many of you like to study this, or to hear something from it? *(Wait for response.)* How would you show that? *(Wait again for answers.)* That's right; you show that you like this book by the way you read it, or by the way you study it in Sunday school, or by the way you listen to it in church.

But sometimes, even though we know we really ought to give this book first place in our time and in our list of things we like to do, other things get in the way. Even these do. *(Show the first items you had.)* Somehow, the word of God gets pushed back into second place. We like it, but other things come first. We want to go on a picnic, or a concert, or play ball. We get mixed up, and when we put them first, we're really showing that they're more important than this. *(Show the Bible.)*

But Jesus didn't want his people to be mixed up like that. He didn't want us to live with the wrong things in first place. So he put this in first place for himself. *(Show the cross.)* When he suffered and died, he was showing us that we're in first place too. And with his forgiveness he takes away our mixed up ideas, and gives us a new power to show how we feel about him. So now we have another question. We're his children. He gave us that place when we were baptized, and every time we hear his word or share his body and blood in Holy Communion he is bringing us back to that place. How can we show it? *(Wait for responses, and then conclude:)* Very good! That's how we show our love for him.

Help Wanted!

SCRIPTURE

After this the Lord appointed seventy others, and sent them on ahead of him, two by two, into every town and place where he himself was about to come. And he said to them, "The harvest is plentiful, but the laborers are few; pray therefore the Lord of the harvest to send laborers into his harvest. Go your way; behold, I send you out as lambs in the midst of wolves. Carry no purse, no bag, no sandals, and salute no one on the road. Whatever house you enter, first say, 'Peace be to this house!' And if a son of peace is there, your peace shall rest upon him; but if not, it shall return to you."

Luke 10:1-6 (Seventh Sunday after Pentecost)

PREPARATION

For this message you will need a bag or a basket, preferably the latter, filled with children's blocks. (Other objects can be used, but blocks are ideal since they will neither break nor roll.) You will also need a large number of small cards, on which names of imaginary children are printed.

This morning I have something in this basket that all of you will recognize, I know. We probably all play with them, because they're so much fun to build with. And today we're going to use these blocks to show you how we build a church.

(As you reach for the first block in apparent intention of beginning the building, tip the basket so that all the blocks will fall to the floor.) Oh! Look at that! All my my blocks have fallen to the floor, and they're all over the place. How am I ever going to have enough time to pick them up? Would some of you help me, please? *(Wait while the children pick up the blocks, thanking them individually as they place them back in the basket.)* Thank you so much; I never would have been able to

pick them all up by myself. You've been real helpers in building the church. *(Place blocks aside.)*

But now let me surprise you. We're not going to build a church out of blocks after all. A church isn't something we make out of blocks, is it? A church is people, people who know about Jesus and believe in him. A church is people like these. *(Show the stack of cards, and begin reading a few of the names.)* These are all people who would like to know about Jesus, but who haven't heard of him yet. *(As you talk, bend the cards so that they will fly out of your hands.)* Oh my! I did it again. First with the blocks, and now with the people's names. Will you help me again, please? *(Wait for the children to pick up the cards.)* Very good! I wouldn't be able to get them all by myself, I'm sure. I really needed your help again.

I still need your help, do you know that? This is the way we build a church. We build it by sharing the good news that Jesus loves us with everyone who doesn't know it. But one person can't do it all by himself; Jesus doesn't even want it to be that way. He sent all his disciples out to tell about him, and so he sends us all to tell *(begin reading some of the cards)* about his forgiveness. No matter how people are scattered out, when all of Jesus' people help in telling them, there will be more and more hearing about him. Just think, you were willing to help build a church by picking up some blocks, and you were willing to help the church grow by picking up the names of those who would be in it. You can also be willing to help really, not just by bringing names back to me, but by bringing Jesus to those whom you name. And after all, when people are scattered away from him, how much better can anyone help than by bringing them back to him? We can really say that's the kind of help we need, and you are the kind of helpers we want, just because Jesus has brought us all back to himself, to build us together around his cross. He's the one who is saying to us "Help wanted!"

The Only Way to Win

SCRIPTURE

And behold, a lawyer stood up to put him to the test, saying, "Teacher, what shall I do to inherit eternal life?" He said to him, "What is written in the law? How do you read?" And he answered, "You shall love the Lord your God with all your heart, and with all your soul, and with all your strength, and with all your mind; and your neighbor as yourself." And he said to him, "You have answered right; do this, and you will live."

But he, desiring to justify himself, said to Jesus, "And who is my neighbor?"

Luke 10:25-29 (Eighth Sunday after Pentecost)

PREPARATION

In the center of a sheet of cardboard, preferably about 10 x 15 inches, draw a rectangle an inch wide and twelve inches high. Divide this into segments of one inch each, as the playing surface for the game which is in this morning's message.

The marker for the game will be a thumbtack, preferably one with a brightly colored head, for visibility purposes. Using the tack, punch a hole in each space before you present the message, since it will make fastening the marker much easier.

From three different colors of construction paper, cut out cards approximately 1 x 3 inches, on which you will print the following instructions:

Set I: Card 1—I read my Bible almost every day.
          Move ahead two spaces.
          Card 2—I help my mother with dishes.
          Move ahead one space.
          Card 3—I shared some candy with my friend.
          Move ahead one space.
          Card 4—I went to Sunday school every Sunday last month
          Move ahead one space.

Set II: Card 1—You never miss reading the funnies, and you watch TV every day.
          Go back three spaces.

Card 2—But you were angry when you did it.

> Go back two spaces.

Card 3—You kept the biggest pieces and just gave him those you didn't like.

> Go back three spaces.

Card 4—But you didn't always pay attention.

> Go back two spaces.

Set III: Card 1—Jesus died to save you; He forgives you!

> Go ahead twelve spaces.

Draw a line across the center of the game board so that six spaces are above and six below. Label this "Starting Point." Mark the very top line of the top space as you hold the board vertically "Child of God."

We have a game to play this morning, one I'm sure you'll find very interesting. It's a game I made up, and I call it "I'm Really Nice." Here's the way we play it:

First of all, I need someone to hold the board for me. *(Choose one of the volunteers.)* All right, Jennie, if you will hold it please, we'll all be able to see it. Hold this side up, so we can all see what it says. This is the *(wait for the children to read the words)* starting point. And way up here at the top is the goal we want to get to, to be the children of God.

Now, the rules are these. Each time I take a card from set No. 1, the set that I call "My own ideas," I move my marker as that card tells me. Then I must also take a card from set No. 2, and do what it says. I call that set of cards "What God knows about me." Finally, when all the cards are gone, I take a card from the last set, where there is only one card. So, we'll move the marker just according to the cards. Does everyone understand? *(Place the marker at the starting point.)* I will need someone to move the marker for me. *(Choose one of the volunteers.)* Good! Now we're ready.

Here's my first card. *(Read it, and as you do, add appropriate comments like "Oh boy! I'm moving ahead already.")* And now I have to take the other card. I wonder how far I'll get to go forward this time. I was able to move ahead two spaces for reading my Bible almost every day. *(Read the other card, and indicate your disappointment.)* Well, that's true, I guess; so I'll just have to go back those spaces. *(Follow this procedure with all the cards from sets one and two, until they are finally used. Your own remarks and involvement will be the key to this part of the message!)* Wow! Here I thought I was a fairly nice person, and would get to the top easily, but look at this; I'm still way at the bottom. I don't think I'll ever make it.

But I have one card left, and I suppose we might as well finish the game. *(Read that card.)* That's really something. Quickly, move my marker all the way up to the "Children of God" line. Jesus loves me and he died for me; that's how I become a child of God. That's really good news too. We can't get there any other way. No matter how many nice things we do, we just can't get out of our sins. But Jesus takes us out of them with his forgiveness. *(As you are saying these words, be indicating the spaces on the game board.)* I might fool myself into thinking that I belong here *(show the upper part of the board)* but really I don't. I belong down here. *(Show the lower part.)* But Jesus came way down here, to bring me way up there. Maybe I have the wrong name for my game. It's really about what Jesus does, and maybe I should call it "He's the only way to win!"

That One Thing

Now as they went on their way, he entered a village, and a woman named Martha received him into her house. And she had a sister called Mary, who sat at the Lord's feet and listened to his teaching. But Martha was distracted with much serving and she went to him and said, "Lord, do you not care that my sister has left me to serve alone? Tell her then to help me." But the Lord answered her, "Martha, Martha, you are anxious and troubled about many things; one thing is needful. Mary has chosen the good portion, which shall not be taken away from her."

Luke 10:38-42 (Ninth Sunday after Pentecost)

PREPARATION

In a large box, place the following items: a baseball, a baseball cap, a swimsuit, a child's snorkel tube or pair of underwater goggles, a piano lesson book, a pitch pipe, a church bulletin, and a Bible (NOTE: If not all these items are available, it is possible to make substitutions, which should be made in pairs. One of the items is always essential; the other is simply desirable, but not necessary.)

Today we're going to pretend that we're doing some different things. In my box I have some of the things that we need, and I'm going to ask some of you to choose the things that you would want to take. Listen very carefully, though, so you choose the right things. I want you to take out the one thing which you really need to do the things we talk about. For example, if we were going to eat some soup, and you had a choice of a fork or a spoon, which would you really need? *(Wait for the answer.)* Of course; we'd all want a spoon, wouldn't we? That's the kind of choice you'll be making. So let's look at our first choice.

Timmy, in my box I have some things for playing baseball. Now I'd like you to pick one thing which you must absolutely have if you are going to play ball. So, look in the box, and take out the thing that you would need. *(If he chooses the baseball, react affirmatively; if he happens to choose the cap, engage him in conversation until he replaces it with the baseball.)* Very good; if we're going to play ball, that ball is really necessary, isn't it?

Tommy, how about choosing something else for us. Let's pretend that you are going to a swimming party. Can you find something in my box that is really necessary; in fact, you wouldn't even go to the party without one, I don't think. *(Wait until he picks out the swimsuit.)* Of course, you need a swimsuit to go swimming at a party, don't you?

Susan, would you like to choose our next thing? Let's pretend that you want to take piano lessons. Of course you have to have a piano, and my box doesn't have enough space for that, but you'd also want something else. See if there is something else you might need. *(Wait for her to pick out the piano book.)* Right! You would want a piano book, wouldn't you? A very good choice.

But now let's look at something else. When Timmy chose the ball, he might also have chosen the cap. *(Show it.)* But he didn't; he knew that a cap is good to have, but a ball is absolutely necessary. That's why he made that choice. And that's the way Tommy chose the swimsuit. He might have chosen this *(show the snorkel or the goggles)* because they are fun to have at a swimming party. But a person must have a swimsuit, first. And it's the same with Susan's choice. A pitch-pipe tells us if the piano is in tune, but we really need the piano book if we're going to learn to play the piano. We don't want to make wrong choices about things like that, do we?

Now we need someone for one more choice. Mary, would you like to choose? *(Pick someone old enough to read well.)* Please choose the one thing that is really necessary if we're going to learn more about Jesus and his love. *(Allow her to make her pick.)* Very good; what did you choose? *(Wait for her answer.)* What was the other item in the box you might have chosen? *(Again, wait.)* Right; it was a church bulletin. *(Turn to the whole group of children.)* Did Mary make the right choice? Of course she did; this is the one thing necessary. *(Show the Bible.)*

Sadly though, we don't always make such good choices. We put other things in first place, things which are fun and good, but things which just shouldn't take first place. This *(the Bible)* is that one thing necessary, because it is the record of how much God loves us, and how Jesus forgives us. But do you know something? He loves us so much that he made us his first choice, and that means we can keep him in first place too, and the word that tells about him.

Our Loving Father

SCRIPTURE

"And I tell you, Ask and it will be given you; seek, and
you will find; knock and it will be opened to you. For
every one who asks receives, and he who seeks finds,
and to him who knocks it will be opened. What father
among you, if his son asks for a fish, will instead of a fish
give him a serpent; or if he asks for an egg, will give him
a scorpion? If you then, who are evil, know how to give
good gifts to your children, how much more will the
heavenly Father give the Holy Spirit to those who ask
him?"

Luke 11:9-13 (Tenth Sunday after Pentecost)

PREPARATION

Place several large stones, or perhaps a small jar of
gravel, in a box which can be covered. In another box
place a carton of salt. In a third box place a cut-out heart,
preferably of red construction paper.

We're all going to do some pretending this morning.
We're going to pretend that we're hungry and we're
going to pretend that we're thirsty. Do you think you
can do that? Let's see!

We'll start off by pretending to be hungry. And the
one who looks the hungriest will get all the food in this
box. *(Show the first box, covered.)* Let's all look hungry;
and I wonder who looks the hungriest. *(Choose one of the
group, preferably one of the older ones who will be able
to cope with the disappointment he might have when he
opens the box.)* So, Denny, here is the food so that you
won't be so hungry. You can even open it and eat it
right now. *(Wait for him to open the box, and then engage him in conversation about it.)* That was a real disappointment, wasn't it? Did you think I'd give you something like that?

Now, I wonder if anyone will want to pretend being thirsty. Let's just try it anyway. The thirstiest one will get to open this box. *(Show it.)* Very good; I think that Pat acted thirstiest. So Pat, would you like to open this box, to see if it's something to take your thirst away? *(Give him the box.)* What's in this box? Will it take away your thirst? Of course not; if anything, salty things make us even more thirsty, don't they? If we were really thirsty, this wouldn't be funny at all, would it? It would almost be mean, instead. And I know one thing; if I did something like this to you, you'd probably never ask me for help ever again.

But now let's look in our third box. This is a different kind of box, because this isn't a trick that I'm playing on you; this is a promise that God is making to you. When we ask him for anything, this is what he promises. *(Open the box to show the heart.)* That's right; I couldn't possibly put enough things in the box for everything that we ask for and that God gives. So I just placed this heart in it. What do you think it is supposed to mean? *(Wait for the answer of God's love.)* Right; it means that whenever we ask for something from God, he always answers our prayers with his love, in one way or another. We don't have to be afraid that he will play tricks on us, because he loves us so much that he doesn't trick us.

That's why Jesus came to the world. He came to show us how much God loves us, and to take away any fear we might have of God. He came to make us God's children, and because we're his children, we can call him our Father, just like we do in our prayers. That's even the way we start the prayer that Jesus taught his children to pray: Our Father, who art in heaven. Let's fold our hands and say that together: Our Father, who art in heaven. And just think, whenever we say those words we can also say "Thank you for being a loving Father."

The Things That Last

SCRIPTURE

And he told them a parable, saying, "The land of a rich man brought forth plentifully; and he thought to himself, 'What shall I do, for I have nowhere to store my crops?' And he said, 'I will do this: I will pull down my barns, and build larger ones; and there I will store all my grain and my goods. And I will say to my soul, Soul, you have ample goods laid up for many years; take your ease, eat, drink, be merry.' But God said to him, 'Fool! This night your soul is required of you; and the things you have prepared, whose will they be?' So is he who lays up treasures for himself, and is not rich toward God."

Luke 12:16-21 (Eleventh Sunday after Pentecost)

PREPARATION

Paste or tape pictures of things children enjoy, such as a bicycle, a toy truck, a baseball glove, an ice cream cone, and a coin on building blocks, one on each. Also tape a cross on a similar block. (Catalog pictures are especially good because they are usually in color; otherwise newspaper advertisements also serve as a source for these pictures.)

Have any of you ever made a tower out of building blocks? *(Wait for response.)* Can someone tell me how to do it? *(Again, wait for answers.)* That's what we're going to do this morning; we're going to build a tower out of these blocks.

But we're going to pretend that this tower is really our own life. Each thing we get that we like very much will be one of the building blocks, just as I have them pasted on these blocks in my hands. *(During this time, the block with the cross on it should not be visible.)* So, let's start building our tower.

I like bicycles very much, so I think I'd probably put the bicycle first; that will be my first building block. And let's see, I always like ice cream, so I'd make that my second one. And my third one might be some money, because

89

I like that. And then maybe I'd put the baseball glove next, and then to top it all, a toy truck. *(As you are saying these lines, match the action to your words.)* There, I have my tower all built; this is my life, with things I like very much.

But now we might have a problem. I'd like my tower to last a long time, because I'd like my life to last a long time, and I want to be happy while it does. But let's look at some of these things. It won't be long, and my truck could get all rusty; that wouldn't be a good building block any more. *(Take it away.)* And I might get too old to play baseball very well, so there goes that building block. *(Remove that one.)* My money won't last forever, so there goes another one. *(Take it off also.)* And when I eat my ice cream, it's gone! *(Remove that block.)* And even my bicycle will wear out someday. *(Take the last block away.)* Now what do I have left of all the things I thought were such important building blocks in my tower? That's right; I have nothing. These things were all good while they lasted, but they just don't last.

So let's look at another building block, the one you haven't seen yet. *(Show the block with the cross.)* Now here is the kind of block which will last forever, because Jesus' love lasts forever. In fact, we have this building block just because Jesus loves us so much. He knew that we would often try to build our lives around these things *(show the other blocks)* and he knew that we would be hurt when they don't last. So he came into the world to give us something lasting. The good news we have this morning, and every day, is that in his love and his forgiveness we have something that will last. He even will be able to enjoy all these other things *(indicate the blocks with the various items)* because we enjoy this *(indicate the cross)* first. And this is the one that lasts. It makes the perfect foundation for our tower. *(Place it at the bottom, and build the other blocks on top of it.)* Just like that!

When The Alarm Rings

SCRIPTURE

"Let your loins be girded and your lamps burning, and be like men who are waiting for their master to come home from the marriage feast, so that they may open to him at once when he comes and knocks. Blessed are those servants whom the master finds awake when he comes; truly, I say to you, he will gird himself and have them sit at table, and he will come and serve them. If he comes in the second watch, or in the third, and finds them so, blessed are those servants! But know this, that if the householder had known at what hour the thief was coming, he would have been awake and would not have left his house to be broken into. You also must be ready; for the Son of man is coming at an hour you do not expect."

Luke 12:35-40 (Twelfth Sunday after Pentecost)

PREPARATION

You will need an alarm clock which can be set to ring while you are speaking. (You may wish to set it off just before you begin, but turn off the bell, so that you can also turn it on at the moment of your choosing.)

It will be necessary to enlist the help of one of the older children before the message is presented. Instruct him to hold up his hand as soon as you begin speaking.

Today we're going to see who is widest awake in our group. Here is what I mean. All of you see this alarm clock, do you not? What you don't know is that it's going to ring some time very soon. And the first person to have his hand up in the air when the alarm rings is the most alert one of the whole group. If we had a prize, we'd give that person a prize, but maybe just knowing that he's the most alert one will be enough. So, remember, whoever has his hand in the air when the alarm goes off, that person wins! (*At that point, the person you have chosen before should hold her hand up.*)

Well, Sarah, your hand is up already. But the alarm didn't ring yet! Why do you have your hand up so soon? *(Permit her to answer.)* Very good; you say you want to be ready all the time. That's a good idea, I think. By putting your hand up right now, you'll surely be ready, won't you? I wonder if anyone else thinks that's a good idea. Everyone who thinks so might hold up his hand, too. *(By holding up your own hand, you will help lead the children to that response.)* Very good; it looks like we all want to be ready for the alarm to ring. *(Sound the bell.)*

And there it goes! And guess what; we were all ready for it! We didn't know just when it would be, so we were ready all the time. We all wanted to be alert. *(Or, we all wanted the prize.)*

Maybe that's not too important when it's just a sort of game in our church this morning, and we're only waiting for an alarm clock to ring. But it's very important when we're waiting for something else. You see, Jesus told us to be ready for his return to our world. Some day he's coming back, and he wants us all waiting and ready for him. That's not just a matter of holding up our hands, but a matter of remembering that he once held up his hands on a cross for us. That's the way we're ready for him to come back, by sharing his word with each other, by studying his word together, and by receiving his body and blood in the Sacrament. Those are the things he uses to make us ready for his return.

But just think, because of them, we can be waiting with real joy for Jesus to come back. That's even better than raising our hands while we wait for the alarm clock to ring.

The Line That Divides

SCRIPTURE
The Lord said: "I came to cast fire upon the earth, and
would that it were already kindled! I have a baptism to
be baptized with; and how I am constrained until it is
accomplished! Do you think that I have come to give
peace on earth? No, I tell you, but rather division; for
henceforth in one house there will be five divided, three
against two and two against three; they will be divided,
father against son and son against father, mother against
daughter and daughter against her mother, mother-in-law
against her daughter-in-law and daughter-in-law against
her mother-in-law."
Luke 12:49-53 (Thirteenth Sunday after Pentecost)

PREPARATION
The only material needed for this message is a piece of
string or rope long enough to establish a division into
two sides of the area in which the message is to be presented.

Have you ever played any games in which you choose
sides? *(Wait for the response.)* What kind of games are
those? *(Again, wait; the involvement of the children in
the conversation involves them in your message, too.)*
That's right; those are games in which we choose up sides,
with some people on one team and some on the other.

Sometimes we divide people other ways. For example,
I have this piece of string in my hand, and I'm going to
ask Andrew to hold the other end and step away from
me. Now we have divided this part of the room into
two parts. I'd like to have all the boys on this side of the
line, *(point to one side)* and all the girls on this side.
(Point to the other side.) Very good; you are now in two
groups, with this little line dividing you.

Of course we could divide another way, too. Let's have
everyone who is in the fourth or fifth or sixth grade on

this side of the line. *(Indicate the side.)* And let's have everyone younger than that on the other side. *(Again, indicate.)* And we've done it again. We have two groups, with our string dividing you.

But Jesus tells us that he is going to make a different kind of division. We can show that, too. Let's have everyone who loves Jesus come over to this side. *(Wait while the children move.)* That's right; everyone of you can come to this side. All of us know that Jesus died for us to take our sins away. He loves us and we love him, so we can be on this side. That's exactly why he came to the world, so that we could all be on his side.

But sadly, there will be some people who don't want to believe all he did for us. They don't care that he died for them, too. They are like people who tell the captain, "We don't want to be on your side." And that's the line that divides people, the line that puts them on the other side, away from Jesus.

That makes us feel sad, of course. We'd like everybody to be on the same side with Jesus. That means we'll want to tell others so they can be on this side too. But just think of the good news we have to tell them. Jesus came to put us all on his side. He wanted us so badly that he even died on the cross for us. He didn't want any line, even the line of sin, to divide us from him.

When The Door Opens

SCRIPTURE

He went on his way through towns and villages, teaching, and journeying toward Jerusalem. And some one said to him, "Lord, will those who are saved be few?" And he said to them, "Strive to enter by the narrow door; for many, I tell you, will seek to enter and will not be able. When once the householder has risen up and shut the door, you will begin to stand outside and to knock at the door, saying, 'Lord, open to us.' He will answer you, 'I do not know where you come from.' Then you will begin to say, 'We ate and drank in your presence, and you taught in our streets.' But he will say, 'I tell you, I do not know where you come from; depart from me, all you workers of iniquity!' There you will weep and gnash your teeth, when you see Abraham and Isaac and Jacob and all the prophets in the kingdom of God and you yourselves thrust out. And men will come from the east and west, and from north and south, and sit at table in the kingdom of God. And behold, some are last who will be first, and some are first who will be last."

Luke 13:22-30 (Fourteenth Sunday after Pentecost)

PREPARATION

From light cardboard, such as file folder stock or oak tag, prepare a castle front by sketching in a few lines to represent large stone blocks. Do this in light colors, since the effect you want with the building is one of brightness and joy. Glitter can be dropped on paste lines to add color to the building.

Make the doors large enough so that they can be cut in the center and at both top and bottom, to be opened. Behind them place a picture of Jesus.

Prepare the following four cards:

1. I give a lot of money to the church.
2. I work hard at the church.
3. I never miss church or Sunday school.
4. Jesus died for me.

I wish that I could draw as well as others I know; this picture would be a lot better then. *(Show the picture.)* What do you think it is? *(Allow the comments to develop as they will.)* That's right; it's a big building. It's a castle; someone recognized it. But this is not just any old castle. I wanted this one to be something really special, because I wanted it to represent something different from a building on earth. I wanted it to look like heaven. But that's why it was so hard, because we know heaven is not just like a castle like this; it's something so huge and so beautiful we can't even draw a picture of it. But let's just pretend that this is heaven, O.K.? And these are the doors. *(Point to them.)* And these are the messages four people sent about getting through those doors.

Here is the first one. It's from Mr. Givesalot, and it has to be first, because that's the way he likes to be. Let's hear what he says. *(Have the card read.)* Well, did the doors open? Of course not; they're just as tightly closed as they were before. Too bad, Mr. Givesalot. Giving a lot is very good, but it doesn't make a person better than another, and it doesn't open the doors of heaven, either.

Here's our second card, and this is from Mr. Worksalot. He really wanted to be first, but Mr. Givesalot got ahead of him, but he does work a lot around the church. I wonder why he thinks the doors should open for him? Let's find out. *(Have someone read the card.)* Did the doors open yet? No? It must be like Mr. Givesalot. Working for the church is very good, but it doesn't put a person in front of others either, and it doesn't open up heaven for us. So let's go on.

Here's our third message, and this is from Mr. Comesalot. He's always in church and in Sunday school; that's why he thought he should get to be first, but the other two pushed him aside. Let's hear what he says. *(Have the card read.)* Well, look at that. The doors still aren't opening. Being in church and Sunday school must be good for a person, I'm sure. But they don't open the doors of heaven.

Let's try our last card. This is from Mr. Sinsalot. No wonder it's the last card. After all, to be a sinner isn't a good thing, is it. No wonder Mr. Givesalot and Mr. Worksalot and Mr. Comesalot all push in front of him. And what does his message say? *(Have the card read, and as the children are reading it, open the doors to show the picture of Jesus.)* Wow! Look at that! He didn't brag about himself at all; he just said "Jesus died for me." And the doors came open. What a surprise!!

But it really shouldn't be such a surprise. After all, that's the reason Jesus came, and that's the way he said it would be. The first would be last and the last would be first, and the only one who can open the doors of heaven is Jesus himself. That's our good news this morning, though, because that's what he does for us.

Bursting With Pride

SCRIPTURE

Now he told a parable to those who were invited, when he marked how they chose the places of honor, saying to them, "When you are invited by any one to a marriage feast, do not sit down in a place of honor, lest a more eminent man than you be invited by him; and he who invited you both will come and say to you, 'Give place to this man,' and then you will begin with shame to take the lowest place. But when you are invited, go and sit in the lowest place, so that when your host comes he may say to you, 'Friend, go up higher'; then you will be honored in the presence of all who sit at table with you. For every one who exalts himself will be humbled, and he who humbles himself will be exalted."

Luke 14:7-11 (Fifteenth Sunday after Pentecost)

PREPARATION

You will need two balloons, of equal size. It will also be helpful to have an adult assist you in blowing one of them to reasonable size, while you continue to inflate yours to the breaking point. (This will require a few experiments, probably. In any event, the balloons should be inflated before using in this message, just to be sure they can be blown up easily.)

This morning we're going to talk about one of the sins that Jesus warns us about very often. It's the sin of pride. I wonder who can tell me what the sin of pride is. *(Permit the children to answer, encouraging several ideas.)* Very good! Now I want you to add an idea I have; someone once told me that the sin of pride is having a big head. *(Motion to your head.)* That means, we think more of ourselves than we ought to.

So I think I would like to show you the sin of pride with these two balloons. They're both very good balloons, and if you look closely, you'll see they're almost alike. They look alike, but they're not quite alike at all. The one Mr. Smith has looks like this one, but it doesn't try to get bigger than it is. Let's watch while Mr. Smith

98

blows up his balloon. *(Inflate the balloon to a fairly large, but still very safe size.)* Very good, Mr. Smith. That's a good balloon.

Oh, oh, I shouldn't have said that. You see, this balloon I have is a very proud balloon. It always likes to think it's the largest, the prettiest, and the best balloon around. It's sort of puffed up with pride, we might say. So let's see what happens with this one. *(Start blowing up the balloon, stopping when it gets about as large as the other one. Then pretend to listen to it.)* Well, my balloon is saying something to me. It's saying "Keep going. I want everybody to know that I'm the biggest balloon." *(Again, inflate the balloon considerably, almost to the point of breaking.)* It's saying something more. *(Pretend to listen.)* How about that; it wants to get bigger yet. I don't know about that, but if it wants to be the biggest,, I guess there's nothing to do but blow it up some more. *(As you blow it up this time, blow it until it breaks, or break it as you are showing it when you stop.)* Oh, now look at that. It wanted to be the biggest and prettiest, and now it's the smallest and ugliest, isn't it. It just burst with pride.

And that's the way the sin of pride works. It makes us think that we're going to be the greatest, but we end up nothing at all. *(Show the balloon.)* And do you know something? There's a little bit of that pride in every one of us. We like to be first or biggest or fastest; we like to have our way. We're often quite a lot too proud!

But that's why Jesus came to earth! He came to people who were filled with their sins of pride, like we are, to take those sins away, too. He came to put his love in their place, to cover them up with his forgiveness. And because he did, we don't have to pretend to be something that we really aren't. He loves us just the way we are, and that means we can like ourselves that way, too. He sets us free from our sins of being proud. So, instead of bursting with pride, we can be overflowing with love.

Our Own Crosses

SCRIPTURE

"Whoever does not bear his own cross and come after me, cannot be my disciple."

Luke 14:27 (Sixteenth Sunday after Pentecost)

PREPARATION

You will need a spool, three short sticks, and one longer stick from a child's Tinkertoy set.
Label the spool Jesus.
Label the sticks with the words "Loving," "Caring," "Helping," and "Sharing."

Today we're going to find out something more about what it means to be a child of God. It means to be like the one who made us his children, Jesus. *(Show the center spool with his name on it.)* And it means to do things like he did. It means to love. *(Place that stick into the spool, to form one arm of a cross.)* It means to care about others. *(Place that stick to form another arm of the cross.)* It means to help and to share. *(Place those sticks, completing the cross.)* That's what it means to be a child of God; it means to be like Jesus. And look at this! What do we have? *(Wait for the answers; there will be no difficulty in recognizing the cross.)*

The problem is that sometimes we don't like to think about doing things for others instead of for ourselves. Sometimes we'd rather be selfish than share. *(Remove that stick.)* Or sometimes we'd rather do things for ourselves than help others. *(Remove that stick.)* And there are times that loving others isn't as natural as being angry with them, and caring about others not as easy as caring for ourselves. *(Remove those sticks.)* But what happened? Now our cross is gone. All we have left is Jesus.

But really, that's not true, either. For if we don't have

the cross, we don't have Jesus, either. We might have him as a teacher or a story-teller, or something like that. But we don't have the Jesus who came just to die on the cross. *(Place the center spool aside, too.)* We really don't have anything left, do we?

And we could even say something else. When we have Jesus with his cross, it means we have our own crosses too. It means that we can care and help and share and give *(insert the sticks again)* because Jesus has done all that for us. When we were baptized, we were baptized into a new kind of life where caring and helping and all those things *(indicate them on the cross)* are the new kind of life we have. With the power that comes from Jesus on his cross, we take up our crosses and live with him.

Finding The Lost

SCRIPTURE

So he told them this parable: "What man of you, having a hundred sheep, if he has lost one of them, does not leave the ninety-nine in the wilderness, and go after the one which is lost, until he finds it? And when he has found it, he lays it on his shoulders, rejoicing. And when he comes home, he calls together his friends and his neighbors, saying to them, 'Rejoice with me, for I have found my sheep which was lost.' Just so, I tell you, there will be more joy in heaven over one sinner who repents than over ninety-nine righteous persons who need no repentance."

Luke 15:3-7 (Seventeenth Sunday after Pentecost)

PREPARATION

For this message you will need a checkerboard, a full set of checkers (both colors) and probably a table on which to place the board. It will also be helpful to use someone to assist you, since moving all the equipment is time-consuming otherwise. If you do not use an assistant, it will be necessary to place a checker in some corner where it will eventually be found.

All of you recognize this, I'm sure. What is it? That's right; it's a game of checkers. And this morning we're going to set up our game, because it will help us understand something about Jesus. So will someone help me set up our checker game? *(Be sure that your volunteer places the checkers for which there is one missing.)*

Now, I'm all set; how about you? Come on, Tim, you're not ready yet. You still have another checker to put down on the board. *(Carry on a short conversation with him about it, pointing out that you cannot play until that checker is found, that your set will be ruined, etc.)*

Well, let's all look around, shall we? I really want to find that checker. *(It should not be too obvious; the lit-*

tle amount of time used in searching will add to the suspense, and if there is conversation, that too will help.) Oh, what did you say, Mr. Smith? You found the checker over there? How about that? *(Your own excitement will carry to the children; if you wish, a small gesture of clapping your hands will invite them to do the same, and their response will make the message more effective.)* Thank you so much! That really makes me happy. Now I have all my checkers again.

It was funny, though, wasn't it? Here I had twenty-three checkers all the time, and I didn't get nearly as excited about them, as I did about finding that one which had been lost.

And do you know something? That's exactly the way Jesus tells us he feels too, when he finds us. He doesn't want us to be lost in our sins, and away from him. He came into the world to look for everyone who had sinned, and that means everyone. He wanted to find us all, to make us his children once again. We just looked around a little for our checker, but he had to give his life to find us But that's our good news today; it's not that we found a checker, but that Jesus found us and made us his own. We're not lost any more; he found us with his cross.

Following The Right Master

SCRIPTURE

"He who is faithful in a very little is faithful also in much; and he who is dishonest in a very little is dishonest also in much. If then you have not been faithful in the unrighteous mammon, who will entrust to you to the true riches? And if you have not been faithful in that which is another's, who will give you that which is your own? No servant can serve two masters; for either he will hate the one and love the other, or he will be devoted to the one and despise the other. You cannot serve God and mammon."

Luke 16:10-13 (Eighteenth Sunday after Pentecost)

PREPARATION

On a sheet of composition paper such as would be used in grade school, write a short paragraph to be entitled "The Life of Christopher Columbus" (or some other topic which might be of interest at the time this message is presented) making sure that the title can be read, even though the body of material may not be. With red marking pencil mark the grade of B— on the paper. You will also need this red marking pencil for use during the message.

Also necessary is a sales slip from some store, preferably with an amount under $1.00 as the total charge. (This can be changed, as long as the material is adapted to make the point that the buyer received too much change.)

Also needed is a cross.

Were you listening to the Gospel this morning? If you were, you probably wondered what Jesus meant, when it seemed that he told a dishonest man that it was good to be dishonest. He didn't mean that at all; in fact, he didn't say that, really. What he said was that the dishonest man would be better off with other dishonest people, as long as he was going to be dishonest anyway. Jesus said that we just can't serve two masters. We can't be both honest and dishonest at the same time.

Of course, none of us are dishonest, are we? But let's look at several things to see how easily we can slip into that sin.

Here is Henry's paper on Christopher Columbus. *(Show the paper.)* It wasn't the best paper in the world, since Henry didn't really work on it very long. He just sort of did it the last minute. But it was good enough to get this grade. *(Show the paper with the B—.)* But Henry knew that his parents wouldn't be happy with that grade, so when the teacher wasn't looking, he picked up the marking pencil, and made just one little change. It wasn't very much, but now look at the grade. The B— has become a B+, and that sounds a lot better, doesn't it? But really, Henry was serving another master than Jesus; he was serving his pride in a better grade, or maybe his fear of being scolded by his parents.

Or here's an experience someone else had. Janie went into the store to buy some thread for her mother. It didn't cost too much, only $.89 *(show the ticket)* and Janie's mother had given her a whole dollar. She even told Janie, "You may keep all the change, dear." That made Janie very happy, but she was even happier when the clerk in the store brought the change. You see, the clerk thought Janie had given her a five dollar bill, so she brought her all that extra change. Janie thought about it a little while, then decided it was the store's hard luck, and her own good fortune, so off she went to spend some of her money, a lot more than she thought she would have. Now, what kind of master was she serving? *(Wait for response.)* That's right; she was serving her selfishness, too, and doing it by being dishonest.

But sins like that are exactly the reason Jesus came. He knew that we would have many opportunities like that, and he knew that the master we call selfishness or the master we call pride or the master we call dishonesty can really take hold of us. But he gives himself to us as a different master. He died on the cross for us *(show the cross)* so that we don't have to follow those other masters at all. Instead we can follow him! He tells us that living his way is something better than living with pride, or living selfishly or living dishonestly. He gives us a new way to live, because we have a new master to follow.

Now, what do you think Henry should have done with his grades? *(Wait for the answer, and if the time permits, allow a short discussion.)* Or what do you think Janie should have done with all the extra money? *(Again, allow discussion.)* Very good! You know what should be done, and the good news is that Jesus gives us the new strength to do it. *(Show the cross.)* He leads us into following himself as our new master.

If He Won't Follow Directions

SCRIPTURE

And he said, "Then I beg you, father, to send him to my father's house, for I have five brothers, so that he may warn them, lest they also come into this place of torment." But Abraham said, "They have Moses and the prophets; let them hear them." And he said, "No, father Abraham; but if someone goes to them from the dead, they will repent." He said to him, "If they do not hear Moses and the prophets, neither will they be convinced if some one should rise from the dead."

Luke 16:27-31 (Nineteenth Sunday after Pentecost)

PREPARATION

You will need a very simple child's game, such as "Blockhead" along with a copy of the rules for the game. You will also need a Bible.

This morning I'm going to tell you a story about our two friends, Timmy and Tommy. They were playing this game. *(Show the game.)* And they started off having a lot of fun with it. *(Demonstrate as you continue.)* Timmy put a piece down, and then Tommy; then Timmy put another one on the pile, and so did Tommy. But then when Timmy was putting his third one on the stack, he knocked the whole thing over. *(Do so yourself, retaining some semblance of care, though, as if you really were playing and it was not an intentional act at all.)* So, right away Tommy started saying: "I won, I won." But Timmy became quite angry. "No, you didn't," he said. "I was putting on a yellow block, and with a yellow block you get another turn." So Timmy built up the stack again, and this time, he managed to make the block stay on.

They kept playing. *(Continue to build the structure.)* But in just a few more turns, Timmy tipped over the stack again. This time he had a different excuse. He said:

107

"I was using a round block, and that means an extra try." But now Tommy wasn't happy. In fact, he was quite angry. "You don't follow the rules," he said, and went to tell his mother.

"Mother, come tell Timmy to follow the rules," Tommy said, "or I'm not going to play with him anymore."

But mother's answer surprised Tommy. "Timmy knows the rules," she told him. "He knows them well enough to know how to play properly, and if he doesn't want to follow them, it won't help if I tell him." And so, very sadly, Tommy and Timmy stopped playing.

You see, Timmy did know the rules; he even had them right there *(show the rules for the game)* if he really wanted to know them. He just didn't want to know what they said; he wanted his own way.

And that's the way many people are about God. They like to make up their own rules about him, to pretend they can have their own way with him. But God gave us something to tell us about him. *(Show the Bible.)* It's not a set of rules about how we can love him, but it's a record of things he has done to show that he loves us. But if we don't want to hear of those things, we will probably just set his record aside. *(Set the Bible aside.)* And that's really sad, because then we miss out on being together with him.

That's why Jesus came to our world, though. He didn't want anyone to miss out on God's love. He suffered and died on his cross to take away from us the sin of doing everything our own way, and from our sins of not wanting to hear of the love of God through his Word. And that's the good news we have; we don't have to do things our own way, we have someone new to follow, the one this book tells us about. We have Jesus, and the new direction of his forgiveness. And that's not only something to follow; that's something to enjoy, always!

A Faith That Grows

SCRIPTURE

The apostles said to the Lord, "Increase our faith!"
And the Lord said, "If you had faith as a grain of mus-
tard seed, you could say to this sycamine tree, 'Be rooted
up, and be planted in the sea,' and it would obey you."

Luke 17:5-6 (Twentieth Sunday after Pentecost)

PREPARATION

Items necessary for this message are a hand exerciser
(or a rubber ball large enough to squeeze if the exerciser
is not available, a light barbell or dumbbell, and a copy
of the Bible.

Today we're going to talk about developing our muscles. After all, we like strong muscles, don't we? And I
have some things here to develop those muscles. *(Show
the three items you have.)* All of these things are to
make our muscles stronger, if we use them properly.

Let's start with this one. *(Show the hand exerciser, or
the ball, whichever one you are using.)* How does this
make stronger muscles? *(Demonstrate its use; with the
ball a repeating squeezing action is all that's necessary.)*
Do you see what I'm doing? How does that make me
stronger? Which muscles do you think it helps grow?
(Allow the children to answer.) Very good; and if I want
stronger hand and wrist muscles *(indicate them)* I'll get
them by using this. Of course, if I think my hands and
wrists are strong enough already, I'll probably just put it
aside, and never use this exerciser at all.

But let's look at something else. *(Show the barbell
set.)* What do we call this? *(Wait for response).* Does
anyone know how to use it? *(Choose one of the children
who answers, and permit him or her to demonstrate.)*
Very good! You knew what to do with the barbell, didn't

you? Now tell me which muscles it makes stronger. *(The children will probably not know the names of the muscles, but can indicate which ones they are.)* That's right; it makes our arm muscles stronger. And we like to have strong arms, don't we? Of course, if we think our arms are strong enough, we'll probably never use something like this. *(Place it aside, with the hand exerciser.)*

Now we'll look at a third muscle builder. *(Show the Bible.)* How would we use this? *(Allow the children to share their ideas about it.)* Very good! We use this when we hear it, or when we study it, or when we read it, or even when we memorize parts of it. That's the way to use it.

But what muscles does this exerciser build? *(Hold the Bible up again.)* Who would like to answer that question? *(Permit one or more of the children to answer.)* That's right; this exerciser develops the muscles of our faith. It's God's way of making us stronger Christians.

Of course, just as we said with these things *(point to the hand exerciser and the barbell)* we might say with this, too. If we don't feel we need stronger wrists and hands we probably won't use this. *(Point to the hand exerciser.)* If we don't want stronger arms we won't use this. *(Point to the barbell.)* And if we don't feel we need stronger faith, we may not use this. *(Point to the Bible.)*

But Jesus did say that if we had strong enough faith, we could move a tree from where it is planted to be planted right in the ocean. How many of us have faith that strong? So, how many of us still need this *(point to Bible)* after all? That's right; we all need a faith that grows! And the good news we have is that when we share Jesus in his word *(point to Bible)* or in his sacrament, *(point to altar)* we know that he is making the muscles of our faith grow stronger. That's the way to exercise for the people of God.

Our Thank-you Notes

SCRIPTURE

On the way to Jerusalem he was passing along between Samaria and Galilee. And as he entered a village, he was met by ten lepers, who stood at a distance and lifted up their voices and said, "Jesus, Master, have mercy on us." When he saw them he said to them, "Go and show yourselves to the priests." And as they went they were cleansed. Then one of them, when he saw that he was healed, turned back, praising God with a loud voice; and he fell on his face at Jesus' feet, giving him thanks. Now he was a Samaritan. Then said Jesus, "Were not ten cleansed? Where are the nine? Was no one found to return and give praise to God except this foreigner?" And he said to him, "Rise up and go your way; your faith has made you well."

Luke 17:11-19 (Twenty-first Sunday after Pentecost)

PREPARATION

You will need five thank-you notes, one of which is to be filled out as indicated in the message below. The other four are to be written out during the course of the message.

Does anyone recognize what I have in my hand? You're right, it's a piece of note paper. But this is a special kind of note. Do you see the word here in front? It says "Thank you." That's because this is a thank-you note. And I really liked getting this thank-you note. It came from friends of ours, when we had sent them a wedding gift. It says: "Dear Friends, Thank you for the lovely candle-holder you sent us for our wedding. It's very pretty, and we have it on our coffee table all the time." Getting that note of thanks made us feel so good about the gift we sent and about the friends we sent it to.

So this morning, we're going to write some thank-you notes, too. So, let's everybody pick something we like especially that we want to say thank you to somebody for. Who's ready with something they're especially thankful to have? *(Allow the children to answer, choosing four of the answers to write out on the thank-you notes.)*

Very good! Susan is especially thankful for her friends, Andrew is thankful for his toys, Timmy wants to say thank you for his clothes, and Denny for his food. So let's write those things in our notes. *(Do so.)* But now we have a problem. Denny, who are you going to thank for your food? *(Permit the answer to come from him. If he says, "My parents," continue with "And where did your parents get it?" Your purpose is to lead every answer eventually to God. On the other hand, if the answer "God" comes too quickly, insist that the children explain why they gave that answer.)*

So now our thank-you notes are complete, aren't they? We have found a lot of things to be thankful for, and someone to thank for them. But I still have one other question. How many of us remembered to thank God for these things yesterday? We had them then too, didn't we? Or how about the day before yesterday? We enjoyed them all that day, too. Maybe that says something about how forgetful we are. We're forgetful when we ought to be thankful.

But even forgetful people have some good news to share, to take us out of our forgetfulness or even out of our sins of not being thankful. Jesus Christ made those very sins his own. In the Gospel lesson today we heard how he healed some men with a very bad sickness called leprosy. With his forgiveness he heals us of our very bad sickness called sin, whether it's a sin of forgetfulness or a sin of not being thankful. We're healed people, and that means we can thank him for everything we have and everything we are, just like we did with our thank-you notes.

Pray and Pray Again!

SCRIPTURE

And he told them a parable, to the effect that they ought always to pray and not lose heart. He said, "In a certain city there was a judge who neither feared God nor regarded man; and there was a widow in that city who kept coming to him and saying, 'Vindicate me against my adversary.' For a while he refused; but afterward he said to himself, 'Though I neither fear God nor regard man, yet because this widow bothers me, I will vindicate her, or she will wear me out by her continual coming!'" And the Lord said, "Hear what the unrighteous judge says. And will not God vindicate his elect, who cry to him day and night? Will he delay long over them? I tell you, he will vindicate them speedily."

Luke 18:1-8a (Twenty-second Sunday after Pentecost)

PREPARATION

Since this message is meant to be shared as a modern story, there is no preparation necessary. (You may wish to use a picture of a new bicycle to illustrate Heidi's wish, and a picture of a portable TV to show Frank's.)

This morning I'm going to tell you a story about two young people, whose names were Frank and Heidi. They are much alike, since both of them wanted something new, and both of them decided to ask their parents for it. First we'll hear about Heidi.

Heidi was a very happy little girl, except for one thing: her bicycle was not only too small for her, it was also worn out. So she thought and thought, and decided the only thing she could do would be to ask her parents about it. That evening she asked them if they would please buy her a new bicycle. They didn't say yes, and they didn't say no. They simply said, "We'll see."

About a week went by, and still Heidi didn't have an answer. So she asked again, only to be told the very same thing. She waited about three days and asked another time. Then she waited just one day, and asked again. Finally, one Saturday she asked at breakfast, and then again at lunch, and then again in the middle of the afternoon. It was then she heard her father say, "I suppose we might as well get her the bicycle now. She needs one so badly that she just keeps on asking for it day after day." You can imagine how happy Heidi was.

Frank had the same kind of experience. He really wanted a TV for his own room, and his parents had told him that when he became twelve years old, he could have one. So when his twelfth birthday came, the first thing he thought about was reminding his parents about the television set he wanted. But he had to remind them again and again, just like Heidi. After all, sometimes parents can be forgetful, can't they? But finally, Frank's parents said "Let's go to the store this afternoon and get his TV. Otherwise he'll just keep reminding us for days and weeks." So, a happy Frank got his TV set.

Now perhaps we should ask a question. Why did you think Heidi got her bicycle or Frank got his television set when they did? *(Wait for response.)* That's right; they continued to ask.

If our parents show their love by finally giving us our requests, how much more will a perfectly loving God listen to the requests we make to him.

Sometimes, though, we get tired of asking. We like God to do things right now, without having to wait for him. That's our sin of impatience. But because Jesus Christ died to take that sin away, too, we don't have to be such impatient people, anymore. We can pray to God because we know him as our loving Father, and we can pray and pray and pray and pray, because we know him as one who promises to hear. We can be patient in our praying, just as Jesus said, and we can live patiently because of what Jesus did.

114

Two Towers

SCRIPTURE

He also told his parable to some who trusted in themselves that they were righteous and despised others: "Two men went up into the temple to pray, one a Pharisee, and the other a tax collector. The Pharisee stood and prayed thus with himself, 'God, I thank thee that I am not like other men, extortioners, unjust, adulterers, or even like this tax collector. I fast twice a week, I give tithes of all that I get.' But the tax collector, standing far off, would not even lift up his eyes to heaven, but beat his breast, saying, 'God, be merciful to me a sinner!' I tell you, this man went down to his house justified rather than the other; for every one who exalts himself will be humbled, but he who humbles himself will be exalted."

Luke 18:9-14 (Twenty-third Sunday after Pentecost)

PREPARATION

For this message you will need six children's blocks, with five of them spelling out the word P-R-I-D-E. The sixth can be blank.

The first five blocks should be labelled on the side opposite the letters as follows:

> P — I sing
> R — I study
> I — I work
> D — I give
> E — I pray

In addition, you will need a cross which can be placed on the other block, to stand higher than the five blocks making the word *Pride*, when they are stacked one on top of the other.

The sixth block should simply have the words "I am a sinner."

This morning we're going to try to show you how some people feel about their faith. We're going to talk about two kinds of people. (*During this time you should have the letters and the labels on your first five blocks hidden.*)

115

This is one kind of person, the kind who is very happy about everything he does in the church. Let's see what he says. *(Show each block, beginning with the letter E, and have the children read "I pray." Continue with all five blocks, making appropriate comments about all of these things being very good things to do, etc.)*

Actually, this man is quite a person, isn't he? He really does a lot of things in his church. Now let's look at this other person, and his block. What does this one say? *(Have the children read.)* "I am a sinner." Well, that doesn't sound too good, does it? This first man really sounds like a better church member, don't you think? *(By phrasing it this way you will probably get a positive response, which is really what you want; your denial of it will be all the more dramatic!)*

No! Not at all! He's not a better church member at all, even though his pile of blocks reaches higher. But let's turn them around to see what they really represent. *(Turn the pile so that the word PRIDE shows.)* What is that word? That's right; it's the sin of pride, the sin we all have, and the sin we all show when we start thinking we're really something in the church.

So now let's look at this other man. All he could say was "I am a sinner." But *(take the cross)* to such a person Jesus says: "You have my forgiveness." *(Place the cross on the block.)* Do you see? Now his tower is higher after all. That's what Jesus meant when he said those who are proud will be humbled, and those who are humble, who are not proud, will be lifted up. And that's what Jesus says to us, too. With his cross he takes away our sins of pride *(with the cross, topple the tower of blocks)* to fill us with his forgiveness as a way to live. *(Place the cross back on the block.)* But do you see, when we build our life in the church with Jesus' forgiveness, we don't have to worry about how tall a tower is. We know how big the cross is, and it's big enough for all of us!

116

The Right People

SCRIPTURE

And when Jesus came to the place, he looked up and said to him, "Zacchaeus, make haste and come down; for I must stay at your house today." So he made haste and came down, and received him joyfully. And when they saw it they all murmured, "He has gone in to be the guest of a man who is a sinner."

Luke 19:5-7 (Twenty-fourth Sunday after Pentecost)

PREPARATION

You will need pictures of several types of people, trying to get as much contrast as possible. One might be the picture of a pastor, such as is found in church supply catalogs; another might be the picture of some socialite, obviously very well dressed. A third might be a picture of some depressed person, or some very dirty person, or even someone on his way to prison.

This morning we're going to look at some pictures of people, and we're going to try to decide some things about them. First of all, let's look at this person. *(Show the picture of the pastor.)* What could you say about him, from this picture? *(Allow the children to comment, directing them to several thoughts such as "He's a religious person," or "I wouldn't be afraid of him," etc.)* We'd probably enjoy being with that person, wouldn't we?

Here's another picture to decide about. *(Show the picture of the socialite, or the wealthy person.)* What do you think you can tell me about this person? *(Again allow the conversation to go on for a short time.)* Yes, I think you're right; this person is probably very wealthy, has fine clothes, and is used to good things. He would be a fine person to have around, too, wouldn't he?

Now, how about this person? *(Show one of the contrasting pictures.)* Or how about this one? *(Show the picture of the person going to jail.)* They're not the same kind of people at all, are they? They aren't as clean, they aren't as wealthy; they don't seem to be as good to have around, do they? If Jesus were going to visit us today, we'd want to introduce him to people like this *(show the first two pictures)* rather than to people like this, wouldn't we? *(Show the last pictures, and with your own actions affirm what you say.)* Right?

Wrong! If that's the way we feel, there's something much more wrong with us than with these people. *(Show the "less desirable" pictures again.)* We look at the outside of people, and sometimes love them just for what we see there. But Jesus looks inside people too, and loves them for the help he can give them there. That's all the difference in the world!

Or maybe we should say that is the difference Jesus makes in the world. He didn't come into the world just to be a loving savior for rich and successful people. He came to be the savior for all people. Jesus knows that every one of the people in the world needs him just the same, whether they have lots of money or just a little, whether they are clean or dirty, even whether they're on their way to jail or to church. He loves them all the same, and he wants all of them to love him the same way, too.

That's the good news we have this morning. If Jesus were to look only at our sins, he would have to say that none of us are the right people for him. Even the way we look at other people makes us wrong. But with his suffering and death, he takes those sins away. And that's what makes us the right people. It's not in what we do for ourselves, but in what he has done for us.

The Dead Are Raised

SCRIPTURE

But that the dead are raised, even Moses showed, in the passage about the bush, where he calls the Lord the God of Abraham and the God of Isaac and the God of Jacob. Now he is not God of the dead, but of the living; for all live to him.

Luke 20:37-38 (Twenty-fifth Sunday after Pentecost)

PREPARATION

For this message, it will be necessary to have two boxes, both with covers, of approximately equal size. Line the inside of one with bright yellow paper, perhaps marking it with a few orange or yellow lines as well. On the inside of the other, fold together a handkerchief, a napkin, or a piece of cloth, to simulate a bed, and place a doll on that bed. Cover both boxes.

Do you remember Easter morning? That was a long time ago, but I wonder how many of you remember it. Hold up your hands if you do. *(Wait for the response.)* Very good! I'm glad you remember it so well, because it's so important to us. I wonder if anyone remembers how we greeted each other on Easter morning. When I said "Christ is risen!" what did you answer? *(Again wait for the response.)* Right! That was our answer! "He is risen, indeed!"

I said that was very important, and it still is. Something great happened that day. The people went to the grave to find the body of their friend *(take the empty box in hand)* but when they got there, what happened? *(Wait for the answers.)* That's it! The stone was rolled away from the door *(uncover the box)* and the grave was empty. *(Show the inside of the box.)* Jesus wasn't dead any longer. He had risen from the grave. It was his resurrection day. That's a long word, isn't it? Let's say it together. Resurrection day. It means the day Jesus came out of the grave.

Do you know that some day we will go to our graves, too? Unless Jesus comes before we die, we'll be in a grave. *(Open the other box, show the doll.)* But do you know something! We don't have to be all worried and afraid of that at all. Look in this box again. I tried to show something like a bed, because that's the way the Bible talks about us when we die. It tells us that we go to sleep, with Jesus.

But it also tells us that we're going to wake up someday! When he comes back, he's going to wake us all from our sleep. *(Open the cover once again, and lift the doll out.)* And we're going to have brand new bodies and a whole brand new life with him and with all his people. He died, and we will too. But he rose again, and so will we. That's what the Gospel lesson meant today when it said that God is the God of the living, not of the dead. We will live forever. And do you remember our Easter word? It was *(say it slowly so the children can join in)* Alleluia! Once more: ALLELUIA!

Courageous Christians

SCRIPTURE

Settle it therefore in your minds, not to meditate be-forehand how to answer; for I will give you a mouth and wisdom, which none of your adversaries will be able to withstand or contradict. You will be delivered up even by parents and brothers and kinsmen and friends, and some of you they will put to death; you will be hated by all for my name's sake. But not a hair of your head will perish. By your endurance you will gain your lives.

Luke 21:14-19 (Twenty-sixth Sunday after Pentecost)

PREPARATION

Necessary for this message are three boxes, to be labeled

1. Some of the time.
2. All of the time.
3. None of the time.

Also necessary are the following cards:

1. I pray before lunch in school.
2. I remind my friends when they use God's name in cursing.
3. I try to be friends with everyone.
4. I tell my friends when they are doing wrong.
5. I remind my friends when they start to gossip that it is sin.
6. I say my prayers when I go to bed, even at slumber parties.

This morning we're going to talk about some of the hard things a Christian faces. Most of the time it isn't so hard, really. No one stops us from coming to church or Sunday school; no one searches our house to see if we might have a Bible there that we are not supposed to have. It's not quite as hard as Jesus said it would become in the very last days of the world, when God's people might even have to go to jail or be killed because of their faith. But still, there are some times it is hard to stand up for our Christian faith.

121

So, this morning I'm going to show you some cards, and we're going to try to put them in the right box. Let's look at our boxes first. They say *(have the children read the labels on the boxes)* "Some of the time," "All of the time," and "None of the time." We'll try to decide in which box each of these cards should fit. No! That's not quite right; we'll know in which box they should fit. But we want to see in which one they actually do fit. We want to be completely honest about it, and tell the truth all the way. So who would like to draw the first card and read it? *(Choose someone, have the person read the card, and if possible make the decision.)*

All right, now we're starting. Susie read "I pray before lunch in school." Now, into which box do you think you would place that card, Susie? *(Allow her to make the choice, placing the card in the proper box.)* I notice that you said "Some of the time." How many would agree with Susie? How many would say "None of the time?" *(Wait for a show of hands.)* How many would say "All of the time?" Let's find out why we have those answers. *(Involve the children in the conversation as to the reason for their choices. Then continue the message with the other cards, following the same procedures. Do not be afraid to have the children participate. It might be necessary at times to say something like "When I was as old as you, I might have been afraid to say something to my friends" etc. The idea to be developed is the recognition that taking a Christian stance is not always easy.)*

So, it seems we have quite a few cards in the "None of the time" and the "Some of the time" boxes, when really they ought to be in the "all of the time" box. I think that shows something. It shows that we might not have to go to jail for believing in Jesus, but we sometimes have to do some hard things because we do believe in him. And sometimes we fail to do those things. I wonder why. *(Again, permit the children to answer, leading to the idea*

122

that sometimes we're afraid of how people will treat us, what they will think, etc.)

That's really it. We have trouble doing all the things we should because we're a little afraid. So I wonder how we can get over being afraid.

But I don't have to wonder about it very long. Jesus told us the way. He gave us his promise to be with us, and that gives us new courage. He said that wherever we are, there he will be, and when he is with us, we don't need to be afraid. He loves us, he forgives us, and he changes us. That's really good news, isn't it? We don't have to be frightened people; we are courageous Christians.

Something to Use

SCRIPTURE

As they heard these things, he proceeded to tell a parable, because he was near to Jerusalem, and because they supposed that the kingdom of God was to appear immediately. He said therefore, "A nobleman went into a far country to receive a kingdom and then return. Calling ten of his servants, he gave them ten pounds, and said to them, 'Trade with these till I come.' But his citizens hated him and sent an embassy after him, saying, 'We do not want this man to reign over us.' When he returned, having received the kingdom, he commanded these servants, to whom he had given the money, to be called to him, that he might know what they had gained by trading. The first came before him, saying, 'Lord, your pound has made ten pounds more.' And he said to him, 'Well done, good servant! Because you have been faithful in a very little, you shall have authority over ten cities.' And the second came saying, 'Lord, your pound has made five pounds.' And he said to him, 'And you are to be over five cities.' Then another came, saying, 'Lord, here is your pound, which I kept laid away in a napkin; for I was afraid of you, because you are a severe man; you take up what you did not lay down, and reap what you did not sow. He said to him, 'I will condemn you out of your own mouth, you wicked servant! You knew that I was a severe man, taking up what I did not lay down and reaping what I did not sow? Why then did you not put my money into the bank, and at my coming I should have collected it with interest?' And he said to those who stood by, 'Take the pound from him, and give it to him who has the ten pounds.' (And they said to him, 'Lord, he has ten pounds!') 'I tell you, that to every one who has will more be given; but from him who has not, even what he has will be taken away. But as for these enemies of mine, who did not want me to reign over them, bring them here and slay them before me."

Luke 19:11-27 (Twenty-seventh Sunday after Pentecost)

PREPARATION

Collect several objects which children recognize and use, such as a box of crayons, a baseball, a tennis racket, etc.

Today I want you to pretend that I'm going to give you something, and I want you to tell me what you're going to do with it. For example, my first gift might be these. *(Show the box of crayons.)* I think I'll give these to Amy, if Amy will tell me what she would do with them. *(Wait for Amy to respond.)* Well, let me ask you a question, Amy. If you really appreciate my gift, what would you do? Right! You'd use it. Perhaps you'd even color a picture for me to show me how much you like it. I know this, if you were to put these crayons in the bottom of your drawer and never take them out, I would think that you didn't like them very much.

I'll give this *(the baseball)* to Chuck, with the same questions. What will you do with this, Chuck? How could you show me that you really like it? That's it! You'd show me by using it, and maybe even asking me to play with you. You certainly wouldn't just stick it away in the storage room, would you?

We could ask those same questions with all the things we have here. These are all things to use, aren't they? *(Name them, and indicate their uses.)* When someone gives us things like these, we show how much we appreciate them by using them, and maybe even by sharing them with the one who gave them to us.

Jesus told a story something like that, the story you heard in the Gospel lesson this morning. He tells us that God has given us many things, our voices, our ideas, our abilities, and so forth. But he doesn't give all those things to us just so that we can hide them away and never use them. What he gives us, he expects us to use. And most especially, he expects us to use them for him.

Maybe that's why we should say that his greatest gift to us is also the easiest to use. It's the gift of his love, and we use it whenever we share it. That's the way it grows and grows, just like the money the master gave people in Jesus' story. And do you remember, the only servant the

125

master was angry with was the one who didn't use the gift at all?

That's something for us to remember, too. Jesus came into the world to bring us God's greatest gifts, his love and his forgiveness. Like all the other gifts he has given us, they aren't meant just to keep to ourselves. They won't grow that way! But just because we do have them, we can use them, in the same way Jesus brought them to us. Just think, all of God's gifts, like these *(indicate the items you have)* and these *(indicate your hands)* abilities, and these *(point to the cross)* are ours to use and share. That's the way they grow!

Our Special King

SCRIPTURE

And he said, "Jesus, remember me when you come into your kingdom." And he said to him, "Truly, I say to you, today you will be with me in Paradise."

Luke 23:42-43 (Last Sunday after Pentecost, Christ the King)

PREPARATION

Prepare pictures to represent a castle, a throne, and a crown. Also, prepare either a picture of a crown of thorns, or fashion one from branches, if available. You will also need a rather large cross.

This is a special day in the church, one we don't often hear about. It's called Christ the King day. So this morning we're going to think about Jesus as our king.

Of course, most of us know what kings are. They are great rulers in some lands. They live in large, large houses called castles. *(Show the picture.)* They sit on a special chair. *(Show that picture.)* I wonder if anyone knows what that's called. Right; it's called a throne, and when the king sits on his throne, people have to do exactly what he tells them. And he even wears a special hat. *(Show the crown.)* It's more than just a hat; it's the sign that he has all the power of the whole kingdom. It's his crown.

But Jesus is a different kind of king. Instead of a castle, he made his home here on earth with us, without even a special house to call his own. This was his crown *(show the crown of thorns)* and it wasn't so much a sign of all his power as it was a sign of all his suffering for us. That's the way with his throne, too. *(Show the cross.)* This was his throne. He really was a special king.

And these very things make his kingdom different and special, too. You see, he didn't come to show such great

127

power over people that they had to obey him in everything; he came because they couldn't obey him. For Jesus the greater power was the power of his love, even for disobedient people. It was a love he expressed by wearing this. *(Show the crown of thorns.)* For Jesus, the way to establish a new kingdom wasn't with a throne full of authority; it was with a cross filled with his forgiveness. *(Show that cross.)* That's the way Jesus became our king.

Of course, there were people who didn't feel they needed his love, so he wasn't much of a king to them, I suppose. And there still are such people. And there were people who didn't feel they needed his forgiveness, so they wouldn't let him be king for them, either. And there still are such people. But there are also people like the one man who was crucified with him, who knew he needed all the love and forgiveness Jesus came to offer him, and to him, Jesus was a real king. He even said: "Jesus, remember me when you come into your kingdom." It's the same thing we say when we remember our sins and how much we need Jesus' forgiveness. And then Jesus says the same thing to us that he said to that man: "Today you will be with me in Paradise." Just think, that's the good news we have. Jesus is our king. With his love and his forgiveness he comes to us, and today we're with him in Paradise because to share these things is to have a little bit of Paradise already. What can we say but "Hail to the King!"